TEACHING READING TO INDIVIDUALS
WITH LEARNING DIFFICULTIES

Second Printing

TEACHING READING TO INDIVIDUALS WITH LEARNING DIFFICULTIES

By

PATRICK ASHLOCK, Ed.D.

Professor of Psychology
National College of Education
Evanston, Illinois
Lecturer in Education, Rosary College
River Forest, Illinois
and
Northeastern Illinois State College
Chicago, Illinois

With Contributions by

WINEVA MONTOOTH GRZYNKOWICZ, M.A.

Professor of Education
National College of Education
Evanston, Illinois
Lecturer in Education, Rosary College
River Forest, Illinois
and
Northeastern Illinois State College
Chicago, Illinois

and

RICHARD L. DERVIN, B.A.

Teacher of Language Arts and Social Studies
Skiles Junior High School
Evanston, Illinois

CHARLES C THOMAS · PUBLISHER
Springfield · Illinois · U.S.A.

Published and Distributed Throughout the World by

CHARLES C THOMAS • PUBLISHER

Bannerstone House

301-327 East Lawrence Avenue, Springfield, Illinois, U.S.A.

© *1969, by* CHARLES C THOMAS • PUBLISHER

ISBN 0-398-03050-2 (paper)

Library of Congress Catalog Card Number: 68-29676

First Printing, 1969
Second Printing, 1974

*With THOMAS BOOKS careful attention is given to all details of
manufacturing and design. It is the Publisher's desire to present books that are
satisfactory as to their physical qualities and artistic possibilities and
appropriate for their particular use. THOMAS BOOKS will be true to those
laws of quality that assure a good name and good will.*

Printed in the United States of America
R-1

Dedicated to the graduate students in

my Bradley University

courses for whom the early

drafts of this book

were written.

Introduction

Dᴜʀɪɴɢ ᴛʜᴇ ᴘᴀꜱᴛ ᴅᴇᴄᴀᴅᴇ the literature on children who have difficulty in learning the basic skills of the three R's has become voluminous, redundant and obfuscating.

Shortly after government funds and interest were focused on mental retardation, it become increasingly apparent that children of normal intelligence also could fail to learn to read, write, spell, and/or deal with numerical symbols. Individuals who were medically oriented recalled terms such as dyslexia, dysgraphia, and dyscalculia; the educationally minded remembered Strauss and the brain-injured child; the psychiatrically inclined strengthened their interest in neurotic or character disorders of childhood; the developmentalists concerned with prevention looked into maturational or developmental lags; and the eclectic philosophers put forth terms such as specific learning disabilities, language disorders, or minimal brain dysfunction in order to deal with the problems. More effort has gone into definitions, semantic argument, and search for etiology than in dealing with the problem per se.

Depending on where such a child lives he may be found in a class for the educationally or neurologically handicapped, a brain-injured class, a class for children with minimal brain dysfunction, or a class for the perceptually handicapped. In some locations he may be dyslexic; in others, he may have a specific reading problem. He may even be found in a class for the emotionally disturbed or for the educable mentally retarded.

The confusion in labeling has created equal confusion in teaching, in administration of school programs, and in the training of teachers and others. Essentially, we are concerned with individuals who can't learn to read. Perhaps educators should refresh their memories on the medical history in this regard.

Although reading disability was first described by physicians, educators have ignored the medical term, dyslexia. This term was suggested in 1887 by the German neurologist, Berlin, to replace "word-blindness," first proposed by Kussmaul in 1877. The neurologists used these terms to isolate a central or aphasic loss of the ability to read as a result of known brain injury. In 1895 the ophthalmologist, Hinshelwood, wrote his classical paper on the subject. The earliest reports on dyslexic children were published in 1896 by Pringle Morgan and James Kerr. Morgan described his 14 year old patient as having "congenital word-blindness." In 1917 Hinshelwood reported on a number of children who had been referred to him because their reading difficulty was considered due to some disorder in vision. This did not prove to be the case. Hinshelwood emphasized the importance of two observations: that there were often several cases in one family, and that their symptoms were closely parallel to those which appeared in adults who had lost the capacity to read because of injury to the brain. Hinshelwood was convinced on the basis of post-mortem examinations that under-development of, or injury to, part of the brain might lead to reading failure. He concluded that any abnormality in the angular gyrus of the left side of the brain in a right-handed person might cause failure in reading. Such abnormality might be due to disease, birth injury, or faulty development. He also said that varying degrees of brain damage or dysfunction might account for varying degrees of reading deficiency.

Following Hinshelwood, attitudes and opinions toward reading disability have oscillated like a pendulum. In the 1920's Apert and Potzl postulated developmental delay of functional rather than anatomic nature and there gradually arose the notion of a developmental or maturational lag to explain dyslexia. In the early 1930's, the American neurologist, Samuel T. Orton, entered the scene. In his book entitled *Reading, Writing and Speech Problems in Children* (1937), Orton stressed that language is a function of the central nervous system and stated ". . . attempts at teaching reading and writing before the age of six years were unprofitable. It may therefore be pertinent to inquire whether the cortices of the angular gyrus region have reached a sufficient anatomical or physiological maturity before this period to make reading and writing practical." In discussing obstacles encountered by certain children in gaining a normal mastery of language, of which reading is one component, Orton also mentioned brain damage as the first and most important factor. After repeated attempts to localize the area of damage he stated, "While no area of the brain can be designated as the center for reading because of the complexity of the symptoms, we can, nevertheless, nominate an area in the dominant hemisphere whose integrity is essential to maintaining a normal reading skill and this critical area for this fraction of the language function is the angular gyrus and its immediate environs."

It is interesting to note that, at approximately the time that Dr. Orton became involved with this problem and proposed the term "strephosymbolia," Monroe came forth with her very important book, *Children Who Cannot Read* (1932). Educators, educational psychologists and sociologists then became concerned with the problem, but their writings rarely refer to the existence of a specific and organically determined defect in reading as taught by most neurologists. Gradually, reading disability became a rather nonspecific condition that could be brought about by a multitude of factors. The multifactorial notion reached a peak when Robinson listed at least a dozen causes or types of reading failure in 1946. It should be pointed out, however, that both Fernald and Gillingham, the authors of the two best known remedial reading techniques, felt that neurological factors were involved. Fernald suggested that the condition was "due to certain variations in the integrated brain functioning involving the same region as that in which the lesion is found in acquired alexia."

Current neurological thinking has been stated succinctly by MacDonald Critchley in his classic little volume, *Developmental Dyslexia* (1964). He stated, "The arguments in favor of the existence of a specific type of developmental dyslexia occurring in the midst of but nosologically apart from the 'olla podrida' of bad readers, may be said to rest upon four premises. These comprise: persistence into adulthood; the peculiar and specific nature of the errors in reading and writing; the familial incidence of the defect; and the frequent association with other symbol-defects." He also pointed out that neurologists do not deny that many cases of failure to learn to read fall outside of their conception of a specific defect.

If we then summarize neurological and educational views among the young illiterates in our schools we may find: (1) children with a familial or constitutional dyslexia ("pure" and uncomplicated by neurological and/or environmental handicap); (2) reading retardation along with other learning and behavioral problems, secondary to brain injury; and (3) reading retardation secondary to psychological, educational, and/or environmental causes. The latter would include anxiety, which can cripple a child, and unrealistic adult expectations in school or at home.

Diagnostic evaluation is a continuing event and involves the concerted efforts of physician, educators and psychologists.

A major focus of our attention should be on developing a battery of teaching (diagnostic, corrective and remedial) techniques that will suit each particular individual's needs . . . and on utilizing and incorporating remedial techniques which have already proven their worth, such as Fernald, Gillingham and Slingerland. In those instances where perceptual-motor training is indicated, we can draw from a large body of useful material dating back to Itard, Seguin and Montessori, from which have derived newer techniques such as Kephart, Frostig, Ayers, etc. This handbook provides for the teacher in a remarkably concise way, the pertinent background information as well as a treasure trove of techniques.

It is unlikely that there is one single method for teaching all individuals. Teachers must have at their easy disposal an armamentarium of methods such as this handbook provides, as well as an understanding of why a specific technique would be best for a given individual.

We must also direct our attention to the *prevention* of learning difficulties. It is possible, perhaps probable, that we are actually creating learning disabilities in many children. Since we insist that children start school at the age of six years, we evidently assume that all six-year-olds are ready to learn the three R's. Since the thirty-five or more children in any given first grade are all taught by one method, either visual or auditory, we evidently assume also that in any given class all children behave in exactly the same way, preferring one and the same sensory avenue for learning. If we do not accept these assumptions, then our behavior in educating young children is, at least, pharisaical—for we start them all at six years, willy-nilly, and then put them through the primary pressure cooker until they emerge at fourth grade, reading or not.

The erroneous but popular notion that most immature or "unripe" six-year-olds will catch up with their classmates during the first two or three years of schooling has not been supported in actual practice.

Proper educational assessment, diagnostic teaching and educational therapy or prescriptive teaching should be established in our schools and continued from kindergarten through the primary grades at least. In every case where a child demonstrates deviation or difficulty in learning, there should be an adjustment in the way he is taught. Kindergarten and primary teachers should be trained to utilize multisensorial techniques, to provide perceptual-motor training in the classroom, and to search continuously for methods of instruction that will fill a particular child's needs, rather than search for ways to make the child fit a particular method of curriculum. For that matter, every child deserves a comprehensive evaluation in the pre-school period in order to determine his state of perceptual organization or "ripeness." Such evaluation can continue through kindergarten and the primary grades. If honestly administered, in principle and practice, a flexible ungraded primary from kindergarten through third grade might help to alleviate some of the learning difficulties. If the ungraded primary is not possible, as deHirsch has suggested, a transition class could be provided for those children who need it, either between kindergarten and first grade or between first and second grades.

If we demand that all children go to school, then we must provide appropriate education for each child, and we must also accept, in practice as well as in theory, the concept of individual differences. We must endeavor to differentiate between the child who provides a teaching difficulty and the child who has a learning disability. This excellent handbook is for teachers who are interested in the assessment of educational needs and the means to promote positive growth in learning through appropriate educational programs to meet those needs—for individuals of all ages.

SYLVIA ONESTI RICHARDSON, M.D.
Learning Disabilities Program
Hamilton County Diagnostic Clinics
University of Cincinnati College of Medicine
Cincinnati, Ohio

Preface

TEACHING READING *to Individuals with Learning Difficulties*
is an attempt to draw together into one handbook the findings
of two fields, remedial reading and special education (learning
difficulties), in an effort to make some of the more usable ideas
in these areas available to a wider range of teachers than has
been done before. The individual with reading difficulties is not
confined to the remedial reading laboratory or to the class for
children with learning difficulties. The individual with reading
difficulties may also be found in the regular classroom—elementary, secondary, or college; he may be the young adult in in-
dustry, the Job Corps, or the armed forces. Learning difficulties
do not always result in *apparent* academic retardation. The
"successful" student or young adult might be even more successful if subtle learning difficulties were corrected.

If all such "subtle" learning difficulties could be discovered,
it is possible that at least one third of the school population
would be found to have some type of learning difficulty as viewed
against the background of our present educational system. Such
an attempt to look at reading difficulties in the light of our present-day educational system necessitates a review of the historical
development of remedial reading and the education of students
with learning difficulties.

The effective treatment of reading difficulties is predicated
upon the recognition of individual differences in learning patterns. As we begin to become more cognizant of these individual
differences, we shall be able more and more to not only correct
learning difficulties but also to work toward the prevention of
them.

PATRICK ASHLOCK

Acknowledgments

I AM INDEBTED TO the following authors and publishers for their kindness in permitting us to quote from their publications: David McKay Company; American Book Company; Holt, Rinehart and Winston; Scott, Foresman and Company; The University of Chicago Press; Appleton-Century-Crofts; Illinois Curriculum Program—Office of Public Instruction; Viking Press; U. S. Government Printing Office; American Educational Research Association; Grune and Stratton; The Syracuse University Press; McGraw-Hill Book Company; Charles E. Merrill Books; Webster Division of McGraw-Hill Book Company; New York Times; The Mills Center; The Reading Laboratory, School of Education, University of Pittsburgh; Educational Testing Service; International Reading Association; Silver Burdett Company; Doctor Vicenta Pacheco Pangalangan; Ginn and Company; Harper and Row; Hunter College Chapter of the Council for Exceptional Children; Houghton Mifflin; Macmillan Company, Singer Division of Random House, and Dr. G. N. Getman.

To my own reading cases and to my graduate students in teacher education courses, I am grateful for sharing with me their special insights into the needs of students with learning difficulties and the needs of their teachers.

For her help throughout the preparation of the final draft of this manuscript, I wish to acknowledge a special debt of gratitude to my associate, Wineva Montooth Grzynkowicz. I am most appreciative to Pauline DePeder for her help with sections of Chapter 5.

I wish to express my special appreciation to my secretary, Mrs. Eleanor Abrath, and to my readers, Fred Abrath, Beverly Zinter, David Cristao, Philip Carava, Robert Sandberg, Anthony Jones, Mrs. Betty True, Mrs. Loraine Valeska, and Carl Grube for the preparation of this manuscript.

P. A.

Contents

TEACHING READING TO INDIVIDUALS WITH LEARNING DIFFICULTIES

CHAPTER 1

The Nature of Reading

AT THE PRESENT TIME, there is probably no field of education
in which there is more confusion concerning methodology and
goals than the field of reading. Too often, we tend to think that
this confusion has come about only recently. We should keep
in mind that differences of opinion as to methodology and aims
have been with us almost from the beginning of formal reading instruction.

Fernald (1943) has noted the conflicting methodological
theories which have been present throughout the history of
reading. The *kinesthetic,* or *tracing,* method has been used since
before the time of Christ. The *word group* method was used in
the East at the time of Christ, perhaps before. The *alphabet*
method, or what is sometimes called the *letter-by-letter* method,
was used in the early schools of Greece and Rome. The *word*
method was suggested by Comenius in the early 1600's. The
phonic method came into use in the middle 1800's.

When any new method was formulated, it soon came into
conflict with already existing methods. At the present time, all
these different approaches are in use and each has its stanch
defenders and equally vehement opponents.

We are all, to some extent, confused by various, and often-
times conflicting, goals of reading instruction. For instance, now
we are becoming greatly concerned with the problems of skimming, scanning, reading (whatever that may be), and study-
type reading. As a first step toward straightening out some of
our thinking about reading, let us turn our attention to some
general definitions of reading itself.

Stern and Gould (1965, p. 7) gave the following definition:
"Reading is the art of extracting the meaning of a text, a meaning transmitted by written or printed characters."

Harris (1961, p. 8) said ". . . *reading is the meaningful interpretation of verbal symbols.*"

Betts (1957, p. 4) gave the following definitional treatment of reading:

> First, reading is a *facet* rather than an isolated fragment of language. If this assumption is valid, then systematic sequences in reading must be validated in terms of general language development.
>
> Second, reading is primarily a problem of interpretation, in the larger sense. The semantic emphasis on reading as "the reconstruction of the facts behind the symbols" must take precedence over the so-called mechanics of reading.

Hildreth (1958, p. 61) said, "Reading thus is the process of giving the significance intended by the writer to the graphic symbols by relating them to one's own fund of experience."

Robinson (1946, p. 7) has given the following definition:

> Reading is commonly defined as "the interpretation of printed symbols." Although this definition places emphasis on the central cerebral processes, the impression or stimuli that give rise to meanings are secured through the visual mechanism.

English and English (1958, pp. 441-442) defined reading as follows:

> 1. The perception of written, printed, or engraved symbols constituting a communication, and the (at least partial) understanding of the conventional meaning of the symbols.
>
>   WORD-NAMING (pronouncing the word), while sometimes mistaken for reading, is neither necessary nor sufficient. The ability to read single or isolated symbols is an improper and partial criterion of *reading* in the full sense, which involves understanding a message of greater complexity.
> 2. The perception of gestures, lip movements, etc., and the understanding of their conventional meanings.

Gray (1948, p. 35) commented:

> While reading is a single operation, we can distinguish four different steps in the total reading process—word perception, comprehension, reaction, and integration—all of which reach back to meaning-background.

Bond and Tinker (1957, p. 19) remarked:

The definition of reading here adopted may be summed up as follows: Reading involves the recognition of printed or written symbols which serve as stimuli for the recall of meanings built up through the reader's past experience.

In summary, all of these definitions deal, in whole or in part, with two basic concepts:

1. Word recognition
2. Comprehension
   a. Literal comprehension
   b. Comprehension in depth

In short, reading might be defined as varying degrees of depth of interpretation of symbols.

Since this book is primarily concerned with teaching children who have reading problems, now let us turn our attention to definitions of *corrective* and *remedial* reading.

Harris (1961, p. 21) said:

When the remedial activities are carried on by a regular classroom teacher within the framework of regular class instruction, the term *corrective* reading applies.

Harris (1962, p. 316) went on to state,

Corrective reading is the term usually employed in referring to giving help to children with relatively mild reading disabilities within the structure of classroom instruction.

Grant and Karlin (1964, p. 10) stated,

A corrective program of reading instruction is one conducted by the classroom teacher rather than by a special teacher. Children in a corrective program have reading disabilities of a lesser degree and with fewer accompanying complications than those who are assigned to remedial classes. As a rule the children in a corrective program have no unusual patterns of reading but frequently have immature reading habits.

McCallister (1936, pp. 66-67) remarked,

A corrective case may be defined as a pupil whose deficiencies may be overcome by group teaching. In actual practice it is difficult to distinguish between these two types [corrective and remedial] of cases as the distinction is largely a matter of degree of retardation.

In summary, corrective reading is concerned with the following types of children:

1. Those who have mild reading problems
2. Those who can be helped significantly by the regular classroom teacher
3. Those who can be worked with in a group situation

Now, let us examine some of the definitions of remedial reading.

Kottmeyer (1959, p. 1) stated,

> The term "remedial" reading is loosely used to describe a wide variety of reading activities. It is commonly contrasted with "developmental" reading, with the implication that "remedial" is at least mildly reprehensible, whereas "developmental" has an aura of pedagogical sanctity. Usually the most apparent difference between the two activities is that pupils are segregated from their classmates for "remedial" instruction, but sit in the same room for a "developmental" reading program.
>
> It seems to me that a pupil becomes a "remedial" case and needs particular help *when he cannot participate profitably in classroom learning activities which involve the use of textbooks.*

McCallister (1936, p. 66) said,

> A remedial case may be defined as a pupil whose deficiencies are of such a character as to require individual instruction. Remedial cases are pupils who will not be likely to make satisfactory progress under conditions of group instruction.

English and English (1958, p. 442) defined remedial reading as "individual or group instruction pointed directly at correcting specific ascertained faulty reading habits."

Good (1959, p. 444) described remedial reading as "individual or group instruction aimed at correcting faulty reading habits and at increasing the efficiency and accuracy of performance in reading."

Harris (1962, p. 316) stated,

> The relatively severe cases of reading disability are called *remedial reading* cases; this implies that they need help which should be given, if possible, by a teacher who has had special professional training for such work, and is outside the regular classroom program. Remedial reading is usually done with from one to

six children at a time. Some schools have special remedial reading teachers who work with these children. A few large school systems have reading clinics in which expert diagnosis and remedial teaching are available.

Harris (1961, p. 21) went on to say,

> When the help takes place outside of the framework of class instruction, it is called *remedial* reading. Remedial reading may be conducted by the regular class teacher with an individual or small group during a special period when the rest of the class is not present; or by a special teacher, meeting with an individual child or small group in school, in a clinic or on a private tutoring basis.

In summary, remedial reading may involve one or more of the following factors:

1. Individual instruction.
2. Group instruction.
3. The regular classroom teacher.
4. A specially trained remedial reading teacher.
5. A degree of reading retardation more severe than that found in a corrective reading case.

As can be seen by an examination of these definitions of corrective and remedial reading, there is no clear distinction between the two. In my opinion, the two terms are overlapping, sometimes ambiguous, and perhaps detrimental to the reading progress of the child. A child with a relatively "minor' reading problem may be placed in a corrective reading class. But this so-called minor problem may be due to some rather serious cause. In such a case, the corrective reading case may spend an unspecified term of frustration in the corrective class and then, hopefully at best, he may finally become a remedial reader.

Any child who has a reading problem should be seen first by a specially trained reading teacher who can describe the reading problem as far as possible, estimate the extent of the problem, suggest possible solutions to the problem, and make the final placement of the child in a suitable instructional program. Actually, it would be ideal if all children who have reading problems could receive at least some of their reading instruction from a professionally trained reading specialist.

BASIC FACTORS IN THE READING PROCESS

Motor Factors

We must keep in mind that the entire organism is involved in the reading process. Kephart (1960, p. 37) has stated, "There is evidence that the efficiency of higher thought processes can be no better than the basic motor abilities upon which they are based."

In relation to reading problems, Sperry, Ulrich, and Staver (1958) studied a number of boys who had learning problems. The authors found that many of these boys had a high need for physical movement. Some of the children found good physical activity outlets outside of the school but not within school. De Hirsch (1951) concluded that the hyperactive child needs an environment which provides for motor activity. It should be noted at this point that many reading cases are hyperactive children. One can only hypothesize that the educational needs of children like these might better be met in a Montessori-type of classroom (Fisher, 1964; Fisher, 1965; Montessori, 1948; Montessori, 1959; Montessori, 1961a; Montessori, 1961b; Montessori, 1961c; Montessori, 1962; Montessori, 1963; Montessori, 1964; Montessori, 1965a; Montessori, 1965b; Montessori, 1965c; Montessori, 1965d; Montessori, 1965e; Rambush, 1962; Standing, 1957; Standing, 1962) where movement is such an integral part of the educational program.

It might be assumed that a child who is in good physical condition will be able to persevere at a task, show less fatigue, and not have as much tension as a child who is physically unfit. Also, it may be that a child who is in good physical condition might possess better gross motor coordination and better eye-hand coordination, which are so necessary for the reading function, than the physically unfit child.

Delacato (1959; 1963; 1966) and Doman and Delacato (1964) have theorized that many reading problems result from brain injury, poor neurological development, and lags in neurological development. These authors have developed a specialized type of treatment to be used with these children.

Some very creative work in the area of perceptual-motor

learning is now being carried on at the Achievement Center for Children at Purdue University under the direction of Newell C. Kephart. Kephart (1960) has gone into considerable detail in giving the theory behind his idea that motor performance is basic to other learning processes.

Luria (1959; 1961; 1963a; 1963b; 1965; 1966) has made significant contributions in this field by calling attention to the importance of speech and motor development in relation to academic performance.

Sensory Factors

It is only common sense to assume that if a child does not see or hear well he may encounter difficulty with reading. Any child who has a reading problem should, as a matter of course, have a visual screening test. Hearing screening should consist of an individual audiometric examination. This can usually be done by the school nurse. In the case where a child fails either the vision or the hearing screening test twice, he should be referred to the appropriate medical specialist for further diagnosis.

Perceptual Factors

Perceptual factors are of the utmost importance in learning to read. Ashlock and Stephen (1966, pp. 17-18) have given the following explanation of the place of perception in learning:

Perception is the mental interpretation of the sensations received from stimuli.

Visual perception is the mental interpretation of what the individual sees.

Auditory perception is the mental interpretation of what the individual hears.

Tactile perception is the mental interpretation of what the individual experiences through the sense of touch.

Kinesthetic perception is the mental intepretation of what the individual experiences through the movements [and positions] of his body.

Appropriate perception has taken place (for our educational purposes) when a child has made a mental interpretation which meets a standard set for his norm group by the society in which he operates. For instance, in our society each letter of the alphabet has only one name, and we expect the "normal" child in the primary grades to learn to call each by its name only.

Inappropriate perception has taken place (for our educational purposes) when a child has made a mental interpretation which does not meet a standard set for his norm group by the society in which he operates. For instance, a school child who recognizes a dog as a horse has made an inappropriate perception.

Our definitions of appropriate and inappropriate perception have both cultural and cognitive implications. Different cultures set different standards for their children. This can be verified by anyone who has tried to give one of our standard intelligence tests to someone from another cultural milieu. Also, we expect that people of different intellectual abilities will differ in the degree of exactness of their perceptions.

Adequate perception is of central importance in the educational process. A perceptual disorder can seriously hamper a child's learning.

Experiential Factors

Betts (1957, p. 303) has said,

A rich background of experiences has several values to the reader: First, reading comprehension depends upon understanding of the things referred to. Other things being equal, reading comprehension, especially *critical* interpretation, is enhanced to the degree that the reader is familiar with the topic under discussion. Second, anticipation of meaning—a significant factor in rhythmical and efficient reading—becomes possible to the extent that there is a clear grasp of the basic concepts.

A child has to begin reading about what he knows about. Serious concrete and vicarious experiential deprivation can make reading comprehension an almost insurmountable task for the child. Whether the child has been read to at home, whether there are books at home, and to what extent the child has had pleasant or unpleasant emotional experiences connected with books and reading all influence the degree of effectiveness with which the child will deal with reading.

The inappropriateness of basic reading materials in the past two or three decades has made reading a difficult task for some children. For instance, it is not easy for the slum child in the first grade to deal with reading concepts concerning the father in the double-breasted blue suit coming home to the little white house with the picket fence, to the family nicely balanced with one boy and one girl, usually having one dog and one cat, and all playing nice little games in the front yard. The slum child may have had an experiential background more concerned with playing stick ball in the streets, playing dodge 'em in the streets, turning over trash cans, and living in a home which may or may not have a father. Due to this, the Detroit Public Schools and other organizations have begun to develop new reading materials which are more in line with the experiential background of some of the special groups of children they serve. Some of these series are the *City Schools Reading Program* (Writer's Committee of the Great Cities School Improvement Program of the Detroit Public Schools, 1962-1965), the *Bank Street Readers* (Bank Street College of Education, 1965-1966), and the Multi-Ethnic Edition of the *New Basic Reading Program* of the Curriculum Foundation Series (Robinson, Monroe, Artley Huch, Aaron, Weintraub, and Greet, 1965).

Not all experiences have to be concrete. In opposition to the commonly held idea that television is detrimental to children's reading performance I think that, in the long run, television has done much to improve the reading performance of children in this country. Through the media of television, children can have vicarious experiences which they might never personally experience in their own lives. Consequently, the youngsters appear to bring to school a much wider experiential background, a larger understanding and speaking vocabulary, and a much more highly developed conceptual level than children who have had no experience with television.

In considering the relationship of experience to reading, we must keep in mind the relationship between the experience and the child having experience. For the slow learner, the further removed the reading material is from his concrete experiences, the more difficult the reading task. For the average child, it does not seem to matter so much whether the experiences are concrete or vicarious—at least at the early reading levels. When dealing with the gifted child, especially at the upper reading levels, the vicarious and emotional experiences of the child have important implications for the the selection of reading material and for the understanding of this material.

Language Factors

Reading is only one facet of language. Reading is like the visible part of the iceberg in the ocean—it surmounts and caps a much wider and broader base called language. Language and thinking are almost inseparable. As the child develops, his language skills and his thinking skills develop hand-in-hand.

The more nearly the child's language experiences out of school correlate with his reading material in school, the easier is the task of teaching the child to read. If English is not spoken in the home, the child entering school usually has a handicap in learning to read. *In such a case, he should usually be taught to speak English before he is taught to read it.* If the type of language the child hears is extremely different from that which he is reading, the slower child may be headed for trouble in reading. In certain parts of the country, language is heavily made up of colloquial expressions. When a child faces a textbook which is written in nice "citified' English, he may have some difficulty in understanding the reading material. Also, if the pronunciation in his part of the country is somewhat different from that of the person teaching the phonics programs, trouble may be in store for the child, and this is especially true if he has poor auditory perception.

WORD RECOGNITION

There are three facets of word recognition:

1. Seeing the word correctly.
2. Saying the word correctly.
3. Knowing the correct meaning of the word.

Unless you are a first grade teacher, or a teacher of the handicapped, it is difficult to imagine the difficulty involved in getting a child to look at, and see, a word correctly. The child is often distracted and loses his place easily. Consequently, he has difficulty seeing the word that the class is working with at a given moment. At a somewhat higher reading level, the child with a learning difficulty often looks so quickly at a word that he often confuses it with a word starting with the same letter, with a word with the same general shape or, although not as commonly, with a word with the same ending.

Saying a word is not always an essential part of word recognition. Certainly, the older reader does not say every word he sees as a preliminary step to knowing its meaning. In fact, at the junior high school levels, vocalization or subvocalization of each word is definitely detrimental to the youngster's reading speed. But at the early level, the child's saying the word is necessary for two reasons: First, so he reinforces the association between the written word and the spoken word. Second, so the teacher can know that the child has correctly recognized the word.

Knowing the meaning of the word is, of course, the final goal of word recognition. It does not matter how well a child can sound out a word if he does not know its meaning. It is the responsibility of the remedial teacher to constantly check on the comprehension of the words that his students are able to pronounce.

COMPREHENSION

There are three basic factors involved in the comprehension of reading material. These are the writer, the written material, and the reader. When a student reads a selection, it is as though he is listening to the author talking.

Thus, the student should get some idea of what the author is about by briefly looking over the material to get in mind the author's plan of organization. The student should try to organize in his own mind how he can best attack, understand, and make use of this material. As the student reads, he should make some evaluation of the possible intent of the author. Why has the author written this material? By what authority does he make his statements?

The reading material is the link between the author and the reader. The linquistic structure that the author uses is most important in helping or hindering the reader in understanding the author's ideas. It is important early in the reading act for the reader to become attuned to the author's style of writing. It is also essential that the student make meaningful use of the punctuation involved in the written material.

The student brings to the reading act three vocabularies: his hearing vocabulary, his speaking vocabulary, and his reading vocabulary. The largest vocabulary the reader has is his hearing vocabulary. He understands more words than he can pronounce or read. The speaking vocabulary is probably the next largest vocabulary in the possession of the young reader. But most important in reading comprehension is, of course, the reading vocabulary. The student, to comprehend most effectively, must use his reading vocabulary to the maximum, making intelligent guesses at words which he is not sure about, and, if he is to read any of this material orally with any show of comprehension, using the dictionary effectively so that he can pronounce the words correctly.

Comprehension can be divided into two large areas, literal comprehension and comprehension in depth. The first involves the reader's exact understanding of the author's meaning. The second involves what the reader has to bring, and to add, to the author's material.

In literal comprehension, the reader uses three basic skills: word meaning, sentence meaning, and paragraph meaning. The word meanings the reader is concerned with involve the most familiar meanings for words, synonyms, antonyms, homonyms, and perhaps the derivation of words. To get full meaning from sentences, the reader must be aware of the structure of sentences, and within this total structure, the reader must recognize the relationships and interrelationships of the words involved. Paragraph meaning centers around many of the same skills as sentence meaning, but the skills are used in a more complex fashion. In the paragraph, the reader must recognize the relationship of the various sentences to each other. He should be able to locate the topic sentence whether it begins the paragraph, comes in the middle, or is the summary sentence. It is also desirable that the student recognize sentences which are used as transitions from one paragraph to another and paragraphs which are transitions from one section of reading material to another.

Comprehension in depth involves not just the meaning of written language, but the student's interpretation of written language. Comprehension in depth also involves the student's appreciation of different types of literary selections. And, for some students, the most important part of comprehension in depth is the personalization of meaning.

In connection with comprehension in depth, Huey (1916, p. 5) made the following statement:

> It [reading] is the noblest of arts, the medium by which there still comes to us the loftiest inspirations, the highest ideals, the purest feelings that have been allowed mankind. . . . Reading itself as a psycho-physiological process is almost as good as a miracle.

In the same vein, Edman (1947, p. 263) has said:

> In reading . . . one can surrender for the time being to the spell of Dostoevsky, so that all life is seen in the agony and division of soul that his novels evoke. One yields to the pessimism of Hardy, or the exuberant comedy of Dickens. Thus, too, can one give one's self to the realm of Jane Austen, or to the robust comic humanity of Fielding. . . .

READING FLEXIBILITY

A great deal of attention has recently been called to what is termed *speed reading*. One of the difficulties of teaching or learning speed reading is that no one can agree on what speed reading is. It may be skimming a selection to get the overall picture, scanning to find certain facts, or just reading quickly. No one has yet successfully set up generally accepted comprehension criteria for what is known as speed reading.

What we need here is the understanding of a more basic term: *reading flexibility*. Reading flexibility means using the rate of speed and getting the degree of comprehension suitable for the reader's purpose and the reading material. Gates (1947, p. 36) has probably given one of the best summaries of reading of this type. He said,

> Among the types of comprehension are ability to read rapidly merely to get a general impression of the content; ability to read rapidly with the purpose of selecting certain information, such as that which answers a specific question; ability to read rapidly to note the outline and organization of the material; ability to read to detect specific details; ability to read very thoroughly for full memory, as in the case of reading to master the directions for

operating a device; reading more slowly with thorough analysis, as in the case of "studying" school lessons; thoroughgoing reading of various types of symbolic or specialized material, such as problems in mathematics and physics. In this group also are included other specialized skills, such as skimming a selection merely to note the "highspots" of thought; rapid analysis of special material, such as a page from a newspaper; reading combined with or alternating with various other activities, as, for example, finding and reading a sentence in a selection that is mainly being given verbatim, reading sentences from one's notes during the actual process of extemporaneous speaking; and various forms of reading, as for example, rereading a chapter in a history book for the purpose of remembering the important items or of reproducing an outline, et cetera.

Betts (1957, p. 73) has summed up the idea of reading flexibility succinctly: "A successful reader is as versatile as an all-round athlete."

CHAPTER 2

The Nature of Learning Difficulties

WINEVA MONTOOTH GRZYNKOWICZ

THE NUMBER OF DIFFERENT areas of special education has been constantly increasing. Those children whose handicap was the most obvious were the first to receive our attention. We have noticed the child whose mentality was quite different from others of the same age group. These we have classified for purposes of special education into two subgroups: those who are trainable, and those who are educable. We have recognized the other extreme and called these children gifted. The physically handicapped child, those with chronic medical problems, and the crippled, are not difficult to identify. Other groups that we have been able to classify are the blind, the partially sighted, the deaf, and the hard of hearing. Special educational services have also been provided for those who have speech impairments.

These classifications left us with many children who obviously needed help, but we did not quite know how to label them. Often, for want of a better term, they have been classified as maladjusted, emotionally disturbed, or culturally disadvantaged.

There is, at present, much interest and almost as much confusion in a new field of special education. The 1965 Annual Convention of the Council for Exceptional Children was dominated by programs on learning disorders. Much is now being published on this subject, but there is little agreement on terminology.

According to Dunn (in Frierson and Barbe, 1967, p. 117) the heightened interest in this group of children is due to the increased number of such children today, the growing sophistication and outspokenness of parents, and the dissatisfaction of parents and professionals alike over placing such children in either the regular grades or in special classes for the retarded.

TERMINOLOGY

The labeling of these unclassified children has given rise to so much confusion regarding terminology that the National Society for Crippled Children and Adults, and the Institute of Neurological Diseases and Blindness have made an attempt to clarify the terminology. In Phase One of this project it was reported,

> A review of selected literature revealed a total of 38 terms used to describe or distinguish the conditions grouped as minimal brain dysfunction in the absence of findings severe enough to warrant inclusion in an established category. . . .

This group adopted the term *minimal brain dysfunction syndrome* and defined it as referring to children of near average, average, or above average general intelligence "with certain learning or behaviorial disabilities ranging from mild to severe, which are associated with deviations of function of the central nervous system" (Clements, 1966, p. 9).

The terms referring to this group of children were listed by Task Force One as follows:

Group I—Organic Aspects

Association Deficit Pathology
Organic Brain Disease
Organic Brain Damage
Organic Brain Dysfunction
Minimal Brain Damage
Diffuse Brain Damage
Neurophenia
Organic Driveness
Cerebral Dysfunction
Organic Behavior Disorder
Choreiform Syndrome
Minor Brain Damage
Minor Brain Injury
Minimal Cerebral Injury
Minimal Chronic Brain Syndromes
Minimal Cerebral Damage
Minimal Cerebral Palsy
Cerebral Dys-synchronization Syndrome

Group II—Segment or Consequence
  Hyperkinetic Behavior Syndrome
  Character Impulse Disorder
  Hyperkinetic Impulse Disorder
  Aggressive Behavior Disorder
  Psychoneurological Learning Disorders
  Hyperkinetic Syndrome
  Dyslexia
  Hyperexcitability Syndrome
  Perceptual Cripple
  Primary Reading Retardation
  Specific Reading Disability
  Clumsy Child Syndrome
  Hypokinetic Syndrome
  Perceptually Handicapped
  Aphasoid Syndrome
  Learning Disabilities
  Conceptually Handicapped
  Attention Disorders
  Interjacent Child

They add,

> With few exceptions, the most striking omission throughout the literature was the lack of attempt at a definition of the terms used or the condition discussed. Although there is a more than ample supply of terminology and characteristics, there is a shortage of interpretative elucidation (Clements, 1966, p. 9).

Bateman stated (1966, p. 94),

> In order to define learning disorders broadly enough to include all the problems currently labeled as such, it is necessary to describe them simply as *those deviations in the learning processes which are associated with an educationally significant discrepancy between apparent capacity for language or cognitive behavior and actual level of language or cognitive performance.*

In a recently published book on learning disorders, Johnson and Myklebust (1967, p. 8) preferred the term *psychoneurological learning disabilities*, indicating that the disorder is in behavior and that the causation is neurological. They stated,

> We refer to children as having a psychoneurological learning disability, meaning that behavior has been disturbed as a result of

a dysfunction in the brain and that the problem is one of altered processes, not of a generalized incapacity to learn. . . . It is the fact of adequate motor ability, average to high intelligence, adequate hearing and vision, and adequate emotional adjustment together with a deficiency in learning that constitutes the basis for homogeneity.

Cruickshank (1967, p. 29) used the term *brain-injured children* and subclassified them into three groups:

> (a) Those with a definite diagnosis of a specific or diffuse neurological injury and who are also characterized by a series of significant psychological problems; (b) those with no positive diagnosis of neurological injury (although such may be suspected by the neurologist), but whose psychological and behaviorial characteristics are identical with those children for whom a diagnosis can be definite; or (c) some children in specific clinical groups such as cerebral palsy, epilepsy, aphasia, mental retardation, cultural deprivation, emotional disturbance, and others whose members show the common psychological characteristics of brain injury and where it is either definitely known or logically suspected that some neurological deficit is present.

The label and the definition chosen by any writer seems to coincide quite closely with his field of specialization. Medical personnel tend to chose a term that is based on etiology. This might be any of the terms included in Group I of the list given by Task Force One. Psychologists seem to choose a term that refers to behavior. Educators seem to have tended toward one of the terms that refer to learning problems.

Frierson (1967, p. 4) proposed a distinction between the terms *learning disorder* and *learning disability:*

> Learning disorder might best designate a known impairment in the nervous system. The impairment may be the result of genetic variation, biochemical irregularity, perinatal brain insult, or injury sustained by the nervous system as a result of disease, accident, sensory deprivation, nutritional deficit, or other direct influence. Learning disability might best designate a demonstrated inability to perform a specific task normally found within the capability range of individuals of comparable mental ability.

There seems to be a need for some label in order that these children will qualify for specialized educational services. The term *learning difficulties* should be applied to those children who have learning problems for which there seems to be a reasonable hope for some degree of successful remediation. The term *learning disability* implies a lack of ability to learn, in which case there is no need for remediation. By implying a negative prognosis, we provide no incentive for the teacher. The word *difficulty* implies a problem that needs correction or remediation and therefore implies a positive prognosis, and by using it we have avoided some of the frightening labels which often add emotional problems to the special class placement. If we must brand these children, it seems sensible to use a term which reduces the stigma to a minimum.

It should be kept in mind that the same child can have both a learning disability and a learning difficulty. For example, the child who, for reasons determined by the diagnostician, will probably never be able to read at a functional literacy level, is still given needed learning experiences by the teacher through a verbal approach—the disability remains uncorrected but the difficulty is ameliorated. The disability is the diagnostician's responsibility to define and delimit; the difficulty is the educator's responsibility to accept and manage.

Perhaps the educator's time is better spent in turning away from taxonomy and toward simple descriptions of characteristics found in this group of children.

CHARACTERISTICS

Some characteristics of children with learning difficulties are as follows:

1. *Perseveration*—the inability to relinquish an activity after it has reached its culmination. There is difficulty in shifting from one activity to another. Children usually are able to dispense with an activity when they have received the satisfaction they sought, but the child who perseverates continues the activity after the stimulus has been reduced or removed. This child may make a page full of the same letter or word. He may persist in doing the same problem over and over. He just cannot stop.

2. *Distractibility*—the inability to concentrate on the appropriate stimulus. When new stimuli are introduced and

selection is necessary, there is too much distraction and the child tries to respond to all the stimuli. This child is distracted by noises, sounds, lights, or objects. He has trouble making choices and seems unable to endure confusion. This often leads to the following characteristic.

3. *Disinhibition*—the inability to control responses to extraneous stimuli. This child tries to engage in too many activities and becomes frustrated because he completes none. This can lead to hyperactivity or hypoactivity.

4. *Hyperactivity*—the inability to control the degree of reaction to stimuli. This child cannot sit still, stand still, or do anything for very long. He seems to have an overabundant supply of energy.

5. *Hypoactivity*—the absence of physical activity. This child sits, stands, or sleeps endlessly.

6. *Emotional instability*—lack of emotional control, as the term implies. This child reacts emotionally with little reason or control. He laughs too loudly, cries too hard, and does whatever he feels like doing with few thoughts of consequences. He becomes too excited or too disappointed. He is apt to have temper tantrums and then be too sorry.

7. *Perceptual disorders*—there are many types of perceptual disorders. There may be a figure-ground distortion. Here the child does not know which to copy from the board—the white marks or the black spaces. There may be difficulty in form discrimination—the recognition of differences in shapes such as between a square and a circle or between the letters *c* and *a*. There may be difficulty in form constancy. The letter on the board may look different to the child when he sees it on paper. There may also be a problem in recognizing forms that have been rotated in space. The child may not know a square as a square if it has been rotated at a forty-five degree angle. There may be a problem in the perception of space and spatial relationships. This is the inability to judge size, distance, boundaries, and the child's own relationship to space. This child is "lost" in space. He

may walk into the door because he did not know how far it was from him.

8. *Motor disturbances*—these may range from poor coordination to cerebral palsy. The disturbance may not be noticed but may still lead to a learning problem. The child may appear awkward and clumsy. He may trip or fall more often than other children in the class. His motor problem may not be evident, but might be discovered through the use of the testing procedures described in Chapter 5.

9. *Speech and language disorders*—difficulties with one or more of the means of communication. This may range from delayed speech or retarded language development to one or more of the "aphasias." The teacher may note a difficulty in communication and suspect poor hearing, defective speech, poor auditory discrimination, lack of understanding of word meanings, or poor association of words with symbols. Johnson and Myklebust (1967) have treated this aspect of learning difficulties in depth.

10. *Conceptual difficulties*—difficulties with reasoning and abstractions. This child seems to think concretely and does not make relevant associations. He does not see the humor in jokes, does not "get the idea" of a story, and cannot "read between the lines."

We could also list inappropriate aggressiveness, excessive talking, destructiveness, social immaturity, insecurity, catastrophic reactions, excessive daydreaming, fatigability, poor retention, unusual irritability, detail consciousness, poor body image and many more—but a complete list of characteristics would be almost impossible to compile since each child seems to contribute more characteristics to the list. Actually, the list will not be complete until we have described the last child with a learning difficulty.

CAUSATION

If we can accept the label *learning difficulties* to include all children with problems in learning for whom there is no classification at present, then we must recognize that the list of causes would be as complex as the list of labels in present use. By using the term *learning difficulties* we are not limited to considering such specific causation as we would be if our label were "brain-injured" or "neurologically handicapped."

Organic damage can include injury or damage to the brain before, during, or after birth. This would include any irregularity in the oxygen supply, prolonged labor, use of obstetrical instruments, Rh incompatibility, rubella, and unusual delivery. Damage can result from unusually high temperatures, diseases, reactions to drugs, and accidents.

Frierson and Barbe group harmful influences that can cause learning problems as follows:

1. Developmental lags.
2. Neurological impairments.
3. Nutritional and chemical imbalance.
4. Experiental deficits.
5. Genetic variations.
6. Sensory losses.
7. Metabolic disorders.
8. Emotional disturbances.

They also stated (1967, p. 8) that "one cannot overlook the fact that some manifest disabilities in learning tasks are related to inappropriate education rather than to impaired learning." I believe this statement to be worthy of elaboration and emphasis.

If we acknowledge the fact that there may be developmental lags, it seems most incongruous that so many primary grade teachers expect the same level of performance from each child in the room regardless of his level of development. We hear first grade teachers complain about children in the class (especially boys) who cannot do the assigned work: "Too immature" is one complaint.

It seems to be a common practice that we should not place these developmentally immature children in a special program unless they are at least two years retarded academically, or unless the parent consents. For some strange reason, many school administrators seem to believe that a magic gap between a poorly established expectancy level and a number on an achievement test (or the parents' lay opinion) is a better basis for determining a child's educational needs than a teacher's professional observations and evaluation.

The unfortunate child who was too immature for kindergarten, and too immature for first grade, may then proceed in orderly sequence through the other grades, remaining too immature if someone does not provide the help he needs. He may even get far enough through our educational system to achieve the status of a high school dropout. Much of this could be avoided.

Learning difficulties are not confined to any particular grade level. Many of the learning difficulties that we see in the upper grades and high school might have been overcome if proper educational approaches had been utilized earlier, but that does not negate the responsibility of the school in providing treatment at any level. The high school student who cannot read well, and is given a failing grade because he cannot write a research paper, has little choice—he is forced to drop out.

Children who have no serious problems may progress through any kind of educational environment with no obvious ill effects, but what might they have accomplished in a different environment? For the child with some type of learning difficulty, an inappropriate educational environment may turn the "difficulty" into a "disability." An inappropriate educational environment may well be the one that allows too much freedom, is too permissive, and provides too much stimulation. The child with a learning difficulty needs structure and, often, a reduction of stimuli. The other detrimental extreme—in which the authoritarian leader expects every child to conform and do the same thing at the same time—can also be an inappropriate environment.

Historically, teachers have blamed parents and parents have blamed each other or their ancestors if the child has a problem. Parents may be the cause, either genetically or environmentally, but the fact remains that the child is here, now, in our class and it is our responsibility to teach him.

Although the study of the etiology of learning difficulties is of interest to us, its greatest value probably lies in the prevention of learning difficulties. Bateman, (1966, p. 98) has listed reviews of the extensive literature on the etiology of learning difficulties. It seems that we have come to believe that we must know the primary cause of a learning difficulty before we attempt treatment. This might be convenient, and there could be an advantage in knowing the primary cause; however, it is necessary for the educator to accept the child as he is now, with all his accumulated problems, and initiate an educational program for the present. Knowing the cause does not remove the problem; treatment is still required. Perhaps if we really understood the seriousness of the diagnosis, we would feel that treatment would be useless, when this is seldom the case.

It would be relatively simple to provide the proper corrective treatment if we could have a nice, neat diagnosis, a listing of the deficits, and a manual to match these deficits with the proper treatment. But while we wait for this to be perfected, we still have the child to teach—he will not wait for the magic formula to be developed.

CHAPTER 3

The Development of Reading Instruction In the United States

AIMS AND OBJECTIVES

T HROUGHOUT COLONIAL TIMES, religious indoctrination was the primary aim of reading instruction, with the Bible, the cate- chism, and the prayer book being the most frequently used reading materials. As we think of the years spent today in teaching a child to read, we are sometimes amazed at the short term reading instruction provided for children in those early times. Butts and Cremin (1953, p. 118) stated,

> For those who were intended to go on to a secondary educa- tion, the elements of elementary instruction were expected to be achieved by the age of seven or eight; for those who were not expected to go further in school, ability to read was probably hoped for by the age of twelve or so. . . . [p. 213] Illiteracy at the time of the Revolution was by no means a social stigma. In the rural farm neighborhoods of America the urgently practical affairs of life claimed most of men's energies. The level of technology was low, and the young could learn the livelihoods of their fathers through apprenticeship, through actually engaging in the tasks they needed to know. With only one white male in seven eligible to vote, the political necessity of education was slight. Generally, the young learned the American Way of life from their community—from the family, the church, and the neighborhood.

After the Revolution, reading material in the schools be- came more moralistic than religious—with the added element of nationalism. The new Americans were determined to culti- vate national loyalty in their children through the medium of reading instruction. Thus, the following couplet from the 1727 edition of *The New England Primer*,

The Royal Oak, it was the tree
That Sav'd His Royal Majestie.

became, in the Hartford edition of the early 1800's,

The Charter Oak, it was the tree
That saved to us our Liberty.

The Civil War marked approximately the middle of the next period in the history of reading instruction. This could be referred to as the period when *meaning* became important in enlightened reading instruction. Horace Mann (1844, p. 116), describing Prussian reading methods of the time, said,

> In every such school, also, there are printed sheets or cards containing the letters, diphthongs, and whole words. The children are taught to sound a diphthong, and then asked in what words that sound occurs. On some of these cards there are enough words to make several short sentences and when the pupils are a little advanced, the teacher points to several isolated words in succession, which when taken together make a familiar sentence, and thus he gives them an agreeable surprise, and a pleasant initiation into reading.

In comparing American reading of the same era with its European cousin, Mann (1844, p. 117) went on,

> Compare the above method with that of calling up a class of abecedarians,—or, what is more common, a single child—and while the teacher holds a book or card before him, with a pointer in his hand, says, *a*, and he echoes *a*; then *b*, and he echoes *b*; and so on until the vertical row of lifeless and ill-favored characters is completed, and then of remanding him to his seat, to sit still and look at vacancy. If the child is bright, the time which passes during the lesson is the only part of the day in which he does not think. Not a single faculty of the mind is exercised excepting that of imitating sounds; and even the number of these imitations is limited to twenty-six. A parrot or an idiot could do the same thing. . . . As a general rule, six months are spent before the twenty-six are mastered, though same child would learn the names of twenty-six playmates or twenty-six playthings in one or two days.

In the early 1880's we see the concept of reading being of cultural value coming into the picture. Literary appreciation and elocutionary delivery became important. Some of the moralistic aims of reading instruction still lingered from earlier times.

Due to the beginning of test construction in 1909, the next few years saw even more stress upon the importance of meaning. The shift from oral to silent reading took place as a result of studies which showed that silent reading produced better reading rates and a higher degree of comprehension than did oral reading.

World War I brought out the fact that many soldiers were not functionally literate. The schools were pressed to make meaning the prime objective of reading instruction.

Smith (1965) has stated that the period from the mid-1900's to the present has been characterized by expanding knowledge and technological revolution. Due to these factors, reading has become of central importance to the individual's survival in society. American society has come a long way from colonial times when illiteracy was "by no means a social stigma." In his message to Congress in January, 1965, President Johnson (1965, p. 20) said,

> I propose that we declare a national goal of full educational opportunity.
>
> Every child must be encouraged to get as much education as he has the ability to take.
>
> We want this not only for his sake—but for the nation's sake.
>
> Nothing matters more to the future of our country: not our military preparedness—for armed might is worthless if we lack the brain power to build a world of peace; not our productive economy —we cannot sustain growth without trained manpower; not our democratic system of government—for freedom is fragile if citizens are ignorant.

MOTIVATION OF STUDENT INTEREST

In colonial times the educator was unconcerned with student interest in reading. The student was obligated to learn in order to fulfill his moral responsibilities. Reading material was religious in content, poor in printing, and crude in illustration—if illustrated at all.

After the Revolution, the aims of reading instruction changed somewhat, but there was still little idea of capturing the child's interest. Motivation arose from secondary presses, such as the need for adult approval.

The next period in reading instruction showed a desire on the part of up-to-date teachers for their students to understand the reading material. This was a genuine step forward in motivating student interest.

With the coming of the concept of literary appreciation, children began to get their first real breaks. Meaningful poetry was added to the curriculum. Illustrations were improved. And a few reading selections of child interest crept into the readers.

Interest in motivating children continued to rise until it reached its peak between 1925 and 1935. During this time, and on into the late 1930's, reading programs of "The Activity Movement" often bowed completely to the whims of children's interests. Basal readers were often dispensed with. No structured plan of instruction was found in many schools. Phonics instruction was often thought of as a holdover from the Dark Ages. The children read about what they were interested in. This interest was often correlated across the board—for instance, a class interest in Indians might bring about a curriculum of Indian stories, Indian arithmetic problems, Indian art work, Indian songs, and so on *ad nauseum*. This bubble burst with the coming of World War II, and the discovery that so many young men could not read.

At the present time, there is much genuine concern on the part of educators about motivating students' interests. Reading material has never been so nearly suited to children's maturity levels. Illustrations have never been so beautiful. Motivational techniques have never been so highly developed. But perhaps the pendulum has swung too far. Now the teacher and the textbook writer come all the way to the child. Who today hears much about student responsibility or the obligation to learn?

WORD RECOGNITION TECHNIQUES

Visual Approaches

The visual approach consists of teaching word recognition primarily through the sense of vision. The visual approach is the most basic, and one of the oldest, methods of teaching reading.

The Alphabet Method

The alphabet and various combinations of vowels and consonants form the basis of the alphabet method. Often the alphabet has been combined with the word method as in the famous Hornbooks first made in England around 1450. In 1532, Marens Schulte in Germany published one of the first ABC books. In colonial times, learning the alphabet was considered to be the first step in learning to read. As found in Benjamin Harris' *New England Primer,* probably printed in the 1680's, the learning of the alphabet was considered to be the basis of reading instruction.

The Word Method

The word method consists of learning whole words as the basis of learning to read, rather than learning isolated letters or letter combinations.

Comenius was one of the first to suggest the word method. The work of Pestalozzi also influenced educators to stress the importance of the whole word approach in reading.

Samuel Worchester was the first American author to suggest the use of the word method. Published in 1840, Josiah Bumstead's book, *My Little Primer,* was the first children's reader based on the word method. In 1846, John Russell Webb published a primer called *The New Word Method.* Actually, the new word method affected only the early stages of reading instruction and was not used in the upper grades. Although the word method came into extensive use after 1840, the alphabet method still continued to be an important approach to the teaching of reading. Toward the end of the nineteenth century, Horace Mann urged that the word method be used. He believed that it was based upon the perception of larger units and seemed more psychologically sound in view of what was then known about children's learning.

Eventually, a widespread reaction began to develop against the word method. In reference to this, Pollard (1889, p. 203) said,

> We are inclined to think the inability of pupils in the higher grades to call words is the legitimate outgrowth of the teaching of

the word method. By this method the word is presented to the child as a whole, and the teacher either tells the child the word, or by skillful questioning leads him to use the word. Later, when phonics have been introduced, the teacher writes the new and difficult words on the blackboard and marks them. The general results of these methods on the mind of the pupil are about the same. He soon learns to think he can do nothing with a new word without the help of the teacher in some way. While he should be learning independence in making out his words, he has learned dependence, and his dependence increases with the increase of difficulties.

The Word Group Method

The word group method was in use in the East at the time of Christ. Prior to the Reformation, children in Europe learned to read from prayer books. Thus, they learned by a word or word group method. In this country around the turn of the century, the sentence and story methods came into being. They were outgrowths of the word method taught earlier. George L. Farnham, in *The Sentence-Method of Reading*, (1895, p. 17) stated,

> . . . *the sentence is the unit of expression.* . . . . The sentence, if properly taught, will in like manner be understood as a whole, better than if presented in detail. The order indicated is, first the sentence, then the words, and then the letters. The sentence being first presented as a whole, the words are discovered, and after that the letters composing the word.

Auditory Approaches

Rudimentary phonic* systems were used in early Greek and Roman schools. In 1790, Thornton, in his *Pronouncing Orthography*, suggested a phonic approach to reading. In 1889, Rebecca Pollard published *Pollard's Synthetic Method, A Complete Manual*. It was the most thoroughgoing phonic approach to reading published up to that time. From 1864 to 1868, Edwin Leigh further developed Thornton's work. In 1869, J. M. D. Meiklejohn proposed a phonic approach which was similar to

Phonetics was the term originally used in referring to the relation between sounds and alphabetic symbols. *Phonics* is the term now more commonly used (Smith; 1965, p. 446). Today, phonetics usually refers to the science of speech sounds. (Schubert; 1964, p. 182).

the "word families" of a later day. The *Beacon Readers*, by James H. Fassett, stressed a highly systemized approach to phonics. The primer was published in 1912 and the first reader in 1913.

But phonics, too, fell upon dark days. Mills (1964, pp. 1-2) said,

> By 1920, there was such a reaction against the phonic approach or any method of teaching specific words that no reputable school would dare promote such techniques. . . These trends gave way to unstructured developmental reading programs which engendered a storm of protest from parents and teachers that the children were not learning how to read.

By the 1930's, phonics, when it was taught, was done on a much more limited basis than formerly and was only a part of one of the different approaches to teaching reading.

Today, however, phonic instruction is a part of almost all total approaches to reading. According to Yoakam (1955, p. 11),

> Not a reputable system of teaching reading exists today that does not give extensive attention to phonetic training throughout the entire primary and middle grades. . . . The writer who accuses the school of doing nothing about phonetics is simply saying things that are not true.

Barton and Wilder (1962, pp. 170-174) said, "Some sort of phonics is universal—not so is some sort of whole-word method."

The present revival of interest in phonics is due in part to the interest of modern educators in the linguistic approach to reading. In 1960, experimental work was begun in London with Sir James Pitman's *Initial Teaching Alphabet*. This alphabet contains forty-four symbols instead of the traditional twenty-six. Each symbol stands for only one sound. This approach is an outgrowth of early alphabet-phonic systems proposed around the turn of the century.

Tactile-Kinesthetic Approaches

Plato, in his *Protagoras* (in Freeman, 1908) suggested one of the early approaches to the tactile-kinesthetic method, "When a boy is not yet clever in writing, the masters first draw lines, and then give him the table and make him write as the lines direct." Horace suggested that children learn their letters by using pieces of pastry made in the shapes of letters. Seneca suggested that the teacher use his hand to guide the child's fingers as they passed over the letters which had already been written for the child to copy.

In the first century, Quintilian (in Haarhoff, 1920, pp. 58-59), in criticizing the idea of delaying teaching until the child was seven years old, said,

> Much can very profitably be done by play long before that. It is a mistake to teach children to repeat the Alphabet before they know the form of the letters. These they may learn from tablets or blocks. As soon as the letters are recognized they ought to be written. Following with a pen the form of letters engraved on ivory tablets is a good thing. After letters syllables must be learnt, all the possible syllables in both languages [Latin and Greek]. After the syllables come words, and after the words sentences. . . . As soon as the child has begun to know the shapes of the various letters, it will be no bad thing to have them cut as accurately as possible upon a board, so that the pen may be guided along the grooves. Thus mistakes such as occur with wax tablets will be rendered impossible, for the pen will be confined between the edges of the letters and will be prevented from going astray.

St. Jerome (in Schaff and Wace, 1893, p. 191) in his letter to Laeta concerning the education of Paula said,

> Get for her a set of letters made of boxwood or of ivory and call each by its proper name. Let her play with these, so that even her play may teach her something. . . . Moreover so soon as she begins to use the style upon the wax, and her hand is still faltering, either guide her soft fingers by laying your hand upon hers, or else have simple copies cut upon a tablet; so that her efforts confined within these limits may keep to the lines traced out for her and not stray outside these.

In the eleventh century, tracing on wax or ivory tablets was used in monasteries for the teaching of writing.

In 1612, Brinsley (in Watson, 1908, p. 167), in describing English schools of that period, said,

> When the young child cannot frame his hand to fashion any letter; besides the guiding of his hand and also showing him where to

begin each letter, and how to draw it, some do use to draw before them the proportion of their letter with a piece of chalk upon a board or table, or with a piece of black lead upon a paper . . . let him take a dry pen that cannot blot his book, and therewith cause him to follow that letter in his copy which he cannot make, drawing upon the copy letter very lightly. . . . Thus let him follow his copy-letter drawing his pen so oft upon it, until he thinks his hand will go like unto it. Then direct him to try with another pen with ink, whether he can make one like to that of his copy.

Locke (in Compayré; 1885, p. 49) suggested,

Get a plate graved with the characters of such a hand as you like best . . . let several sheets of good writing paper be printed off with red ink, which he has nothing to do but go over with a good pen filled with black ink, which will quickly bring his hand to the formation of these very characters, being first showed where to begin, and how to form every letter.

Combination Approaches

In the first century, Quintilian (in Haarhoff, 1920, pp. 58-59) suggested "learning the sound and the form of the letter simultaneously. . . ."

In colonial times in this country, the *New England Primer* combined visual and alphabet approaches to the learning of reading. McGuffey, (1879) in the preface to his *Eclectic Primer* stated, "The plan of the book enables the teacher to pursue the Phonic Method, the Word Method, the Alphabet Method, or any combination of these methods."

In Ward's readers, published in 1894, the author tried to reconcile the word method and the phonic method.

Montessori, (Fisher, 1964; Fisher, 1965; Montessori, 1964; Montessori, 1965a; Montessori, 1965b; Standing, 1962) in her multisensory approach established a basis for a combination of teaching methods.

In 1943, Fernald published her *Remedial Techniques in Basic School Subjects.* She developed a method which utilized the auditory, visual, tactile, and kinesthetic approaches to reading.

Mills (1964, p. 15) has summed up the status of teaching word recognition at the present time as follows:

In present day instruction, we find all the various methods described above in use in the classrooms throughout the United States. The selection of the method is generally left up to the whim of the individual classroom teacher. Since there is little or no research data that would indicate the superiority of one method over another, the teacher generally relies on the following criteria in selecting a method or methods to employ: The method by which she was taught to read; the method proposed by the manual that accompanies the basal series that she uses; the method indicated by the principal or supervisor; or the method outlined by college training instructors.

There is little continuity found from one grade teacher to the next in the public schools in a plan for the teaching of reading; therefore, we may find many cases of large gaps in the child's reading skills. For example, if the first grade teacher has been sold on the phonic method as the major emphasis and the second grade teacher attempts to steer clear of anything remotely concerned with phonics, we can readily appreciate the predicament of the child under such a system. He would have little chance for continuous development essential to becoming an independent reader in such a program.

Comprehension

In the latter half of the nineteenth century, attention began to be called to the importance of comprehension—at least in the upper grades. The term *comprehension* was probably first used in Webb's introduction to his third reader in 1856. From the time of the introduction of testing into the reading field around 1910, the importance of comprehension has steadily increased to the present day.

Silent versus Oral Reading

Oral reading was virtually the only type of reading instruction given in the schools in this country during colonial times and almost up to the time of the Civil War. The following quotation from Webb (1856, p. 9) shows how the idea of silent reading began to become important about this time:

> The reading lesson should be carefully read, silently, previous to the class exercise, at which time every word not understood should be examined in the dictionary, and these definitions,

or their import, given at their *spelling* exercise from the *reading* lesson.

Mirick (1914) said,

By far the larger part of the reading done in the world is silent reading. This common, everyday sort of reading is a very different process from oral reading, and has a different purpose. The great majority of people seldom have occasion to read aloud. And yet for many years the only kind of reading recognized as *reading* in the schools has been oral reading. This almost exclusive practice of oral reading in school has produced several results which students of school practice have adversely criticized.

As noted by Smith (1965, p. 159) the period between 1918 and 1925 saw "an exaggerated and, in some cases, almost exclusive emphasis upon silent reading procedures." Smith (1965, p. 160) went on to state,

During the years 1915 to 1918 Mead, Oberholtzer, Pintner and Gilliland, Schmidt, and Judd, all conducted investigations which indicated the superiority of silent reading over oral reading both in speed and in comprehension. . . . A common inference is that as soon as school officials begin to test some phase of instruction, teachers begin to emphasize that phase in their teaching. This was undoubtedly the case in regard to silent reading.

Theisen (1921, p. 8) said,

The tenacity with which primary teachers have clung to oral reading is probably due to two causes. They know of no way to bring about improvement in oral reading except through oral reading, and they have not known how to conduct silent reading exercises.

Coleman, Uhl, and Hosic (1925-1927, p. 7) gave the following summary of the oral versus silent reading conflict:

In the primary grades, before many basal words have been learned, and when recognition of words and phrases is slow, oral reading has especial value. This value resides in the fact that at this stage of reading development the pronunciation of words does not impede the rate of reading; also, oral reading at this stage provides a simple check upon the pupil's accuracy of visual perception and enunciation. By the time the fourth grade is reached, however, the process of recognizing many basal words has been fairly well mastered and has become more rapid than the process of pronunciation. At that stage of reading, therefore, oral reading impedes the rate of reading, and silent reading must be relied upon for rapid reading. While recognizing the value of oral reading in the drill work of the primary grades, the teacher should not overlook the value of silent reading for the same grades. In general, silent study should precede oral reading. Furthermore, the prime importance of silent reading in later school and adult activities commends it to teachers as an essential process for all grades.

THE DEVELOPMENT OF REMEDIAL READING IN THE UNITED STATES

Between 1900 and 1910 this country saw its first studies of reading difficulties. Most of these studies were carried out in the field of medicine. The term *congenital alexia* was coined to describe reading cases that could not be explained in any other way.

The first use of the term *remedial reading* was probably in the article, "The Use of the Results of Reading Tests as a Basis for Planning Remedial Work," written by W. L. Uhl in 1916. The first book on remedial reading, *Deficiencies in Reading Ability: Their Diagnosis and Treatment* was written in 1922 by Clarence T. Gray. Pangalangan (1960, p. 125) noted an early criterion for the selection of remedial reading cases, "Any child . . . who, according to the teacher's judgment, was not making normal progress in reading was qualified for placement in a remedial class regardless of intelligence quotient."

Concerning the early development of remedial reading, Pangalangan (1960, p. 149) said:

> From 1920 to 1939, the following predominant objectives in remedial reading instruction in the elementary schools in the United States were discernible: improvement of fundamental reading skills and abilities, stimulation of a greater desire to read, and personality development. Reading rate and comprehension were the principal areas of emphasis. In silent reading, stress was laid on the elimination of lip movement, development of word attack skills, vocabulary building, and the improvement of the ability to organize, to grasp the main thought, to reproduce material read, and to locate information.

As early as 1925, Gray wrote, "There is urgent need for

teachers who are trained to engage in diagnostic and remedial work more effectually."

Pangalangan (1960, pp. 78-85) gave the following reasons for the development of remedial reading:

1. "One factor was the strengthened holding power of schools." Children no longer dropped out of school in the elementary grades. More poor readers stayed in school longer.
2. "In the 'good old days' teachers did not concern themselves with individual differences in reading." With the change to emphasis upon individual differences, the need for remedial reading became evident.
3. "The migratory nature of the population of the United States played a part in the upsurge of remedial reading programs." This situation brought together children with many different cultural backgrounds. Remedial education was needed to fill the cultural-educational gaps.
4. "Another influence behind the emphasis upon remedial reading is attributable to the mental hygiene approach in education." Educators became aware of how damaging to a child's personality development a reading problem could be.
5. "Another influence that blazed the trail for the wave of remedial reading instruction was the results of research investigations in child development." It was shown that individual children's maturation and learning rates vary widely. Remedial instruction became necessary for those who developed more slowly than average.
6. "The testing movement was perhaps the foremost force which brought remedial reading into reading programs." It was only after educators could measure reading retardation that they became so much concerned about it.

Concerning the continued historical development of remedial reading instruction, Pangalangan (1960, pp. 205-206) said,

Remedial reading instruction in the elementary schools in the United States during the period extending from 1940 to 1949 was primarily concerned with a three-pronged objective consisting of the development of fundamental reading skills and abilities, personality development, and the inculcation of the desire to read for pleasure. Among the reading skills, reading rate and comprehension, including the ability to select the main thought, to note details, to outline, to organize, to retell a story, and to follow directions, received major attention. Other points of attention were vocabulary building and improvement of word attack skills.

In 1937, Samuel T. Orton published his major work concerning the theory of cerebral dominance as applied to reading problems.

Betts, in his *Foundations of Reading Instruction,* was the first to describe the informal reading inventory as a means of judging a child's level of reading performance. This inventory is now frequently used by remedial reading teachers.

In 1943, Grace Fernald's book, *Remedial Techniques in Basic School Subjects,* was published. In this book Fernald described her years of experience in diagnosis and remedial teaching.

In the last fifteen years a number of studies in remedial reading have centered around the emotional problems of children who have reading problems. Studies have indicated that parental attitudes of hostility and intolerance are sometimes present when a child has a reading problem. A variety of psychotherapeutic approaches have been developed for the treatment of remedial readers. *Bibliotherapy* has been developed as a means of helping a child solve his emotional problems through the use of selected reading materials.

During this same period, those interested in the physiological aspects of reading difficulty have been concerned with total neurophysiological development, birth defects, and especially brain damage. Children suffering from sensory and perceptual disorders have been the subjects of studies. Some work has been done concerning teaching children who have aphasia.

Delacato (1965a; 1965b; 1966) and Doman and Delacato (1964) have proposed a very specialized approach to the reading problems of children suffering from brain damage, or immature or impaired neurophysiological development. Kephart (1960) has given a thorough analysis of the motor basis of perception and related learning skills. Perception has become a central factor in the study of reading difficulty cases.

In 1966, Ashlock and Stephen suggested the use of the term *educational therapy* as an organizational concept to include diagnostic, counseling, and training techniques to be used before the student begins remedial instruction.

In Pangalangan's dissertation, *A History of Remedial Reading Instruction in Elementary Schools in the United States,* she has made note of a number of practical approaches to remedial reading instruction. Because of their simplicity, originality, and directness of approach, a number of examples are cited:

> Teacher-prepared booklets which consisted of phrases cut from old primary readers and pasted on each page of the booklets for phrase drills proved to be effective aids in increasing silent reading rate. For a foreign child, summaries of discussions given by the child himself and written by the teacher on the blackboard, became the oral reading material. Advertisements from magazines were sources of words for vocabulary booklets kept by some children. Prose selections from old readers, magazines, and papers were mounted on cardboard and used as material for improving various reading skills.

> .   .   .   .

> For a boy who lacked phonetic ability, phonics lessons were provided for a month. These lessons consisted of learning phonograms presented in the following manner. A word which was meaningful to the boy because it was familiar to him or was of special interest to him was introduced as a keyword. After the phonogram had been encircled, the boy and the teacher cooperatively made a list of as many words as they could think of containing the phonogram. A record of words reviewed and errors made was posted each day.

> .   .   .   .

> Pupils whose silent reading rate was hampered by lack of knowledge of mechanics were taught ten phonetic rules of pronunciation. One type of seatwork given consisted of ten sheets of paper and each sheet contained one phonetic rule. In the course of their reading, pupils looked for words to which these rules applied.

> .   .   .   .

> Poor silent reading comprehension caused by failure to get the meaning of long, unfamiliar words was counteracted by a study of prefixes, suffixes, and stems. Homonyms were studied, too. A seatwork exercise which consisted of fitting words in a paragraph from which several words had been left out was provided for the

purpose of enlarging the meaning vocabulary.

The ability to reproduce material read was developed through short prose selections or poems cut from old readers, magazines, and papers mounted on cardboard. A pupil who received a selection was directed to read it once carefully and silently after which he was asked to reproduce it in writing. In cases of unsatisfactory reproduction the pupil was allowed to read the selection again with the aim of seeking the ideas he failed to note in his first reading. He gave a second reproduction after his second reading which was scored and compared with the first. [Techniques used in the Stoughton Schools, Wisconsin. Excerpts from Pangalangan, 1960, pp. 90-91, 93-94.]

A special group was formed for mirror readers who were given particular drills. Mirror words were written on paper and a mirror was used to show how the reversal was made. The pupils learned the importance of recognizing the initial sound in the word as well as the sequence of letters as they wrote the word, sounded the word as they wrote it, and stressed the initial sound. Mirror words were listed on the chart and the pupils sounded them and pointed to the letters from left to right. [Technique used in the Montefiore Special School for Problem Boys, Chicago, Illinois. Excerpt from Pangalangan, 1960, p. 110.]

Instructional aids employed were unlabeled books of a lower grade level, the dictionary, in connection with the study of hard words, and in the primary grades, words beginning with *a, b, c,* and so on through the alphabet.

.   .   .   .

In the primary grades one teacher discovered children who were capable of helping others. While the teacher worked with one group the rest of the class worked in pairs, the faster helping the slower. [Techniques used in the Fair Street and Pryor Schools, Atlanta, Georgia. Excerpts from Pangalangan, 1960, pp. 111-112.]

Pictures from magazines were utilized in the kinesthetic method of teaching remedial readers, supplemented by textbooks and supplementary readers. Children in the remedial group helped in the accumulation of magazines. They spent about an hour each day for three days a week writing stories about pictures they found in the magazines. Textbooks and supplementary readers were used during the remaining days.

Each child was given the option to pick out the picture that fascinated him, took it to his seat, and wrote a story about it. He learned the spelling of the words he wanted to use in his story through the kinesthetic method. The teacher wrote each word for him. He pronounced the word, traced it with his finger, and said it as he traced it. He went through the same process until he could spell the word correctly from memory. [Techniques used in the Aberneathy School, Portland, Oregon. Excerpt from Pangalangan, 1960, p. 113.]

Individual and group remedial work involved chiefly the re-construction of language units into reading material. The child dic-tated a story to the teacher who printed it as he observed and which he read and re-read as it moved forward. As soon as the child could read the story it was reduced to fragments—first into sentences, then into phrases, and finally, into words. Then difficult phrases were singled out and read in isolation. Lastly, words which the child was liable to meet in succeeding stories were introduced to him, mixed with other words similar in structure. [Technique used in Greensboro, North Carolina. Excerpt from Pangalangan, 1960, p. 128.]

Vocabulary background was built through a lot of discussion and plenty of word-association work, much of which was oral followed by reading. Word addition exercises, related and unrelated word exercises, and a copious amount of "editorial" work proved useful. In "editorial" work, short paragraphs were made more inter-esting through the substitution of more picturesque, more lively, or more realistic words. [Techniques used in Brookline, Massachusetts. Excerpt from Pangalangan, 1960, p. 136.]

Pictures mounted on tagboard were displayed around the room. There were more pictures than there were pupils and several pictures on the same topic; for instance, four pictures of birds, three pictures of kitchens. Each pupil was given a description that he read silently and then tried to locate the picture described. When all pictures had been matched each child proved that he had the right picture. [Technique described in the Harris Report. Excerpt from Pangalangan, 1960, p. 175.]

The problem of lack of interest in silent informative reading and inability to choose significant material for note taking was solved through the game, "Quiz the Teacher" in which the pupils took turns asking the teacher questions on a story they had read. Later the children set up team quiz sessions. [Techniques described in McCormick's Report. Pangalangan, 1960, pp. 223-224.]

Songs were used in a unique manner. Songs with interesting themes focused on the children's phantasy were specially written for reading lessons. As soon as the children had learned these songs, they were presented in a reading situation by duplicating and converting them into reading materials. The children read their copies as they sang. [Technique used in Public School 618, Bellevue Psychiatric Hospital, New York City. Excerpt from Pangalangan, 1960, p. 234.]

This chapter has been a brief overview of the history of reading instruction in this country. For the reader who is interested in pursuing the subject further, it is suggested that he consult the following:

1. Fernald's *Remedial Techniques in Basic School Subjects.* Parts of this book give some of the historical antecedents of the different types of word recognition techniques used today.

2. Mills' *The Teaching of Word Recognition.* In this manual of directions for Mills' *Learning Methods Test,* a history and much of the revelant research concerning different types of word recognition techniques are presented.

3. Smith's *American Reading Instruction.* This is the classic study of the history of reading instruction in this country. Sections are included concerning the history of remedial reading instruction.

4. Pangalangan's dissertation, *A History of Remedial Reading Instruction in Elementary Schools in the United States.* This is a very well done report of the development of elementary school remedial reading instruction in this country. Many of the techniques used should be of great interest to the modern remedial reading teacher in his everyday work.

CHAPTER 4

The Development of Instruction for Children With Learning Difficulties in the United States

RICHARD L. DERVIN

EARLY SPECIAL EDUCATION

THE TERM, *modern education,* is somewhat of a misnomer insofar as it has its basis in concepts that have been developed, hashed over and revised for centuries. What has been done in the United States has been done with the knowledge that children from ancient times onward were indeed fortunate to receive any education at all, and if they were unfortunate enough to have a disability of any type, were liable to drastic consequences. The ancient Spartans killed any child with an abnormality; Europeans, during the early ages, used idiots or freaks as court jesters and, as recently as the middle of the twentieth century, children in Nazi Germany, born with the stigma of being Jewish or with a mental or physical defect serious enough to impair their efficiency for the state, were eligible to suffer very harsh penalties.

While these inhuman attitudes were prevailing in certain quarters, other men were thinking of and devising, methods to help these "unfortunate" children have a more meaningful, rewarding and contributive life. In such climates as these, special education was born and from special education came breakthroughs in the methods of educating the normal child.

Programs for teaching children with learning difficulties have their beginnings in these early programs for special education. Ideas, methods and techniques evolved from these programs to show educators that the child with average or near-average intelligence could profit greatly from these same procedures. According to Doll (in Trapp and Himelstein, 1962, p.

24), "Periere," in working with deaf-mutes, "viewed all the senses as modifications of the primary sense of touch, and believed them all capable of indefinite intellectualization. He used the intact senses educationally to reinforce or replace the damaged, also strengthening the latter by special exercises." This feature corresponds directly to one of the basic tenets of teaching the child with learning difficulties, e.g., teaching to his strengths rather than his weaknesses.

This principle was extended to areas of endeavor as well as points of strength. John Duncan (in Kirk and Johnson, 1951, p. 97) believed that "all mentally handicapped children seemed to have better intelligence in the concrete field—that is, in dealing with things—than in the abstract field which deals primarily with verbal intelligence. Consequently, the curriculum for the mentally handicapped should be taught primarily through a medium of exercises with things that can be handled, seen, touched, or heard, rather than through a medium of words, i.e., the verbal and the abstract." From this concept and others like it, later educators were able to see that any child learns through a variety of media, each contributing to a specific area of learning.

Working with the severely handicapped was one thing, identifying them was another. Doll (in Trapp and Himelstein, 1962, p. 31) informed us that, in what was a predominantly medically-controlled field, mental deficiency was invaded by a psychologist. Alfred Binet, after identifying central intelligence, "supplied a scientifically reliable means for evaluating intelligence which opened new vistas in clinical diagnosis, classification and educational planning." Here again we see the relationship between the evaluation of the mentally deficient and the present-day need for evaluating and identifying the child with the learning difficulty. Doll (in Trapp and Himelstein, 1962, p. 29) also referred to H. B. Wilbur, who pointed out the direction that those in the area of learning difficulties should pay heed to—the matter of "standardized description and analysis of the educational path for better evaluation, prognosis and training." And, this author might add, descriptions in the language of the lay person and not in the professional rhetoric so often found.

Individual differences have had much lip service paid to them over the decades but, often as not, they have taken a back seat to the interests of efficiency and practicality. Warnings have continually been extended to avoid the lumping together of certain groups and then treating them as a mass. This fault exists even among the professionals working with mentally retarded children as evidenced by Luria's (1963, p. 197) warning that "It would be incorrect to think that mentally retarded children (child-oligophrenics) form a homogeneous, undifferentiated group and that it is not possible to find different degrees of defect and different types of disturbance."

Authorities should not be criticized too harshly for the early attitude that the handicapped, especially in the area of retardation, were confined to a rather general class. It was only after the compulsory education laws were passed in the latter half of the nineteenth century in the United States that the schools in this country found more and more mentally retarded children in attendance (Kirk and Johnson, 1951). Prior to this, it would be safe to assume that these children had either left school quite early or had simply never attended.

Public opinion, or rather attitude, was very important in these early days of special education. Prior to, and during the 1920's, an ever-present and increasing view of the threat to society by these individuals classified as feeble-minded was held by the general public. This view was a major factor in establishing confinements for these people, such as asylums and prisons, which would appear to be one cause for the inadequate knowledge of the numbers of such persons.

Since such an opinion was lacking in statistical evidence, it was inevitable that studies would be conducted to test its validity. "Healy and Bronner in 1926 found only 13.5 per cent of juvenile offenders clearly mentally deficient, 9.1 per cent borderline subnormals" (Doll, in Trapp and Himelstein, 1962, p. 43). This encouraged others to investigate this view of the suspect mental defective and seek other causes of juvenile delinquency. "Both William Healy and Pearce Bailey maintained that among the retarded, as among the normal, environment was probably as potent a causative force for delinquency as was mentality." (Doll, in Trapp and Himelstein, 1962, pp. 43-44). This led to a segregation of institutions with different programs for the defective delinquent in some states. It also showed that there were difficulties among the normal as well as the defective and another field of study was in the process of being born, that of the emotionally disturbed.

EARLY ORIENTATION TOWARD PROGRAMS
FOR CHILDREN WITH LEARNING DIFFICULTIES

Programs for children with learning difficulties are not new—just the term as we know it now. These programs have had their roots in older, specialized programs or methods of education for children with learning problems. What is new is the compilation and meshing together of all the phases which benefit the type of child we are discussing into one integrated program, and the offering of a more specialized skill in treating his problems.

One of the early problems that gave an impetus to treating the normal child as an exceptional case was the finding of learning problems among the gifted. The gifted have historically been neglected in the public schools and have either developed through their own efforts, or through private tutors. Some of the biases directed toward gifted children which have in turn created learning difficulties have been:

> The children are bright and will therefore get along well on their own. . . . They should go right along with average children lest they get the impression that their intellectual superiority is something that entitles them to privileges. . . . A third bias is probably more rooted in fact: we frequently do not know how to enrich their educational programs. . . . [Phillips, Wiener, and Haring, 1960, p. 113].

The problems that arise from this neglect are manifold and have even at times disguised the bright child as one needing remedial work.

Remedial instruction has served as a strong argument for programs in learning difficulties. Children who experience much difficulty in skill subjects or subject areas have often had to depend on the classroom teacher for help. When the grade level deficiency has not been too great, this method has been satisfactory, but for a child who has fallen significantly below grade level, for whatever reason, it is usually outside the realm of possibility for the classroom teacher to help the child to any appreciable degree.

To illustrate this problem, two areas might be considered; spelling and mathematics.

It is the opinion of Ashlock and Stephen (1966, p. 62) that most poor spellers can trace at least part of their difficulty to a lack of phonic skills. For remedial work, the teacher should be aware of whether the child has an auditory problem or not. Too often, remediation has been recommended for a child when such remediation only reinforced the child's problem. If the student has a hearing loss due to central deafness, the child may hear sounds, but be unable to interpret them. Placement of this child in remedial work is at best hopeless, and the anxiety caused by failing a subject no one should fail is immeasurable.

In the area of mathematics, Ashlock and Stephen (1966, pp. 63-64) believe there are four main causes of difficulty:

1. Inadequate learning of the basic arithmetic facts and operations.
2. Reading difficulty in connection with story problems and directions.
3. Inadequate perception of spatial relationships.
4. Carelessness.

Whatever the cause, the child must be viewed in terms of having a learning difficulty and be treated accordingly.

Remedial instruction has been very useful in helping the slow learner. The future of this phase of education in relation to programs for children with learning difficulties will be discussed later in this chapter in the section on prognosis.

The minimally brain-damaged child has been the subject of many discussions and evaluations. In every class, there will probably be a child with a learning problem.

> The first step in approaching any problem is to determine its nature. In the case of the child who appears otherwise than normal, this requires a diagnosis by experts who include the physician . . . and the psychologist. If the child is found to have been

brain-injured, the next step is an evaluation by experts of what his potential may be. To what extent can the child be educated to become reasonably self-sufficient and competent as he matures? [Lewis, Strauss, Lehtinen, 1960, p. 8].

This child may or may not appear normal. If he does appear normal, often as not he will remain in the regular classroom. It would be ideal if children who do not appear normal were treated as was mentioned in the preceding paragraph, but "In most school systems, brain-injured children of borderline or below normal intelligence are not differentiated from retarded children who are not brain-injured" (Lewis, Strauss, Lehtinen, 1960, p. 118).

This is definitely harmful educationally to the child as Lewis, Strauss and Lehtinen note in their book, *The Other Child* (1960, p. 119),

> . . . where the school program does not deal with the Other Child's specific learning difficulties, his progress tends to be poor, his performance inadequate and his behavior troublesome.
>
> This conclusion is based on our observations of the progress of children who were enrolled in the Cove Schools, a private school for brain-injured children at Racine, Wisconsin, and Evanston, Illinois, and in a class in the public school system in Joliet, Illinois, which was taught according to methods developed at The Cove Schools.

A child may experience a learning difficulty through a breakdown of the developmental process of the perceptual-motor abilities. ". . . perception is defined as the ability to recognize stimuli. [and] . . . the capacity to interpret and identify the sensory impressions by correlating them with previous experiences. This . . . is a process that occurs in the brain. . . ." (Frostig and Horne, 1964, p. 7). These breakdowns should manifest themselves early in the child's schoolwork by poor achievement in the academic areas or difficulty in learning.

In order to determine where a particular point of breakdown has occurred, *The Purdue Perceptual-Motor Survey* (Roach and Kephart, 1966) was constructed. Part of this survey was first presented in Kephart's (1960) *Slow Learner in the Classroom*, and was later expanded from the original ten tests to the present twenty-two scorable items. "Basically, the survey subtests or items can be divided into three major sections: those concerned with some aspect of laterality, with directionality, and with the skills of perceptual-motor matching" (Roach and Kephart, 1966, p. 3).

Once the area has been pinpointed where the breakdown has occurred, specific exercises may be given to improve the child's perceptual-motor learning. These tests or items can be also used as exercises themselves.

The types of children that have been mentioned so far have been specific examples. One factor that seems to be universal among these children is the factor of injury to the mental health of these children. While a child may have started out with a particular learning difficulty or disability, he may well end up emotionally disturbed. At this point, he will have to be treated as such.

A few experiments in working with these youngsters have been tried. Peter (1965), in his report of Haring and Phillips' (1962) study noted that experimental classrooms using the structured approach made significant gains over the control groups (permissive approaches and an adapted or modified curriculum) in academic achievement and behavior.

According to Smith (1961), the Devereux Schools have used programmed materials with emotionally disturbed children and the results were encouraging.

One salient feature does stand out in the argument for having special classes for the emotionally disturbed. "Starting to teach a special class for the disturbed children should be different from starting a regular class because most of the children have had traumatic experiences at school and with groups (Peter, 1965, p. 153).

The foundation and establishment of special education programs has been encouraging. However, because of these programs' variety, an element of complexity regarding terminology, philosophy, categorization, etc., emerged that often prevented a harmonious and cooperative attitude from prevailing. It is only in recent years that an attempt has been made to produce an educational cement to tie these areas together. This effort is called educational therapy.

EDUCATIONAL THERAPY

"Educational therapy is a concept which encompasses the findings of these disciplines [e.g., special education, psychology, remedial teaching, medicine, etc.] while dedicating itself exclusively to the educational problems of the child who has difficulty learning academic material" (Ashlock and Stephen, 1966, p. xi). In educational therapy, we begin to experience a phase of education totally dedicated to *education*. Delimiting the related disciplines not only presents a clearer picture of what difficulties a child may be experiencing, but also what realistic expectations can be hoped for. Since the educational growth of a child should be the basis of the educator's interest, all other disciplines should serve to clarify, aid, or remove obstacles to this educational growth.

Once again, we can see foundations of this phase of education in early special education. Seguin, in his work with the mentally deficient, recognized one of the primary ingredients of educational therapy—*build-up*. "He [Seguin] suggested that each day's work begin and end with pleasurable activities, and that the intervening tasks be adapted to the mood of the hour" (Doll, in Trapp and Himelstein, pp. 27-28). This concept, linked with other factors of educational therapy, may prove to be very effective in working with children with learning difficulties.

According to Doll (in Trapp and Himelstein, 1962, p. 29), Seguin also preceded modern educational therapy in his views on discipline: "Recognizing the love of the retarded for routine, he based discipline on order. . . ." Once again, borrowing from Seguin, who had such a strong influence on Montessori, teachers of children with learning problems see the need for order and firmness, in order to generate the best possible atmosphere for learning. Only in the security of a regulated climate can a child hope to experiment and strike out on his own. This security (authority) allows the child to realize the safety of a cushion to fall back on when he makes an error, thereby giving him the needed confidence to try again.

"A child needs educational therapy when his level of academic achievement is significantly below his academic potential, and when he is not able to benefit from remedial instruction alone" (Ashlock and Stephen, 1966, p. 6). Using this concept, programs for children with learning difficulties can select children from the general academic program, and, with a *specialized* program, hope to rehabilitate the child's attitudes toward learning and give a fresh concept of himself as a learner.

So many children with learning difficulties are treated, or rather untreated, within the general framework of a class of "average" children. Teachers who are trying to teach to the mythical norm can only hope to spend a part of each day, if that, on a child with learning difficulties and the inevitable results are another year wasted, with the problem being passed on to another teacher.

What of the child who is earnestly making an endeavor to learn? Even though some educators might feel that this child can profit from his experiences in the regular classroom and should be given every opportunity to do so, this is at best, a debatable premise. This situation may be true in some cases, but more often than not, this same child has received more than ample opportunity to profit or succeed and has only increased his frustration and anxiety. According to Peter (1965, p. 153), "A disturbed child's anxiety makes him more likely to fail. In many cases the harder he tries, the worse he does. It is essential that the child be successful from the beginning in a special class." And according to Wattenberg (1955), school children tend to have more emotional disturbances during puberty, which would seem to scream out for early identification of these children so as to prevent later learning difficulties.

If the help these children need so much is best found in the special class, then which special class should they be assigned to? In the first place, unless this child's problem is of extreme severity, he cannot go into the usual special classes because of his normal or near-normal intelligence. The fact of continued failure is not sufficient, nor should it be, to warrant placement in a retarded class, and the situation exists where there are not enough classes geared to each type of problem; the rationale often being that there are not enough of these children to warrant such an *expenditure*.

Bower (1961) found that 10 per cent of school children

were disturbed to the extent that they were in need of psychiatric help. If we can accept this figure, then the number of children who are desperately in need of specialized educational help, over and above this figure, is staggering. This opens the need for concern for having special classes that are equipped with professionally prepared teachers to help these youngsters with learning difficulties.

TERMINOLOGY

There has been an historic struggle among authorities to classify children for the purpose of providing better educational programs for them. This desire for classification has often been selfish insofar as each authority was only thinking of his own area. According to Kirk and Johnson (1951, p. 3), "Children with low intelligence have been of interest to numerous workers—physicians, psychologists, educators, sociologists, geneticists, and others—and each has evolved his own classification, concepts, and terminology."

This has often been the washed-out bridge that has impeded the progress of various members of each of these groups in exchanging and communicating ideas with each other. An example of this obstacle was when Sarason and Gladwin (Sarason, 1959, p. 404) considered mentally retarded as those children who have a higher intellectual level than the mentally deficient, but who are usually culturally deprived, and who "presumably do not have any nervous system pathology." The medical diagnostician may find this consideration of some importance, but the educator does not take great heed of this type of distinction. The teacher finds it much more helpful to delineate degree rather than cause of defect. Since education, especially special education, has had its roots in medical-psychological orientations, it is no wonder that we are overcome by their terminology.

This terminology had a justifiable beginning when Binet and Simon (1914, p. 146) stated, "The essential thing is for all the world to understand that empiricism has had its day, and that method of scientific precision must be introduced into all educational work, to carry everywhere good sense and light."

Binet (in Jenkins and Patterson, 1961) was dismayed by the difficulties of imprecise terminology that existed in describing the mentally defective child. A description of a child differed according to which doctor wrote the prescription. Because of this, there was no way of evaluating the progress of a child from the time of entry into a school until the time of departure. The evidence was strong even in Binet's time that a great need existed for a "standardized description" so that the separate disciplines could take note of and proceed according to what each found.

Doll (in Trapp and Himelstein, 1962, p. 22) used the term *mental deficiency*

> . . . to designate a specific type of mental retardation, (1) developmentally manifest, (2) based upon structural defect, and (3) such as to render the individual socially incompetent. Such *deficient retardation*, being caused by inferiority or maldevelopment of the central nervous system, is irreversible. The failure of some writers to distinguish between mental deficiency so defined and *nondeficient retardation* stemming from sensory impairment, emotional involvement, environmental deprivation, or delayed development has produced much confusion in diagnosis and prognosis.

Doll's last two terms themselves may have caused some workers in the field of learning difficulties a small measure of distaste because of the medical and etiological orientation of these terms.

Kephart (1960, p. 122) makes reference to a dichotomy of terminology in the field—learning problems (learning difficulties) versus learning disabilities. According to Kephart, when a child has a learning problem, he has not experienced sufficient motor learning. If he has a learning disability, he has a medical or physiological reason for his impairment and should be referred for medical treatment.

Kephart has alluded to a distinction in terminology; Ashlock has delimited the distinction (Ashlock, 1968). This finer distinction is that a learning disability is an educational problem for which there is no apparent solution at this time. A learning difficulty is a term applied to an educational problem for which there is a pretty good possibility of at least a partial solution.

The difficulty of telling the players without a scorecard, or a description without a multivolume dictionary, is increasing rather than decreasing. Even the comparatively new term *educational therapist* is coexisting with the term *educationist* (Stephen, 1967, personal communication). An urgent need for a precise and understandable vocabulary is needed for clearer understanding among the many disciplines. This need is made even more urgent by the sudden and much needed emergence of parents into the field.

PARENTS IN THE FIELD

In the field of education, parents can either be great allies or severe opponents to proposed educational programs. If they are the latter, it is often done unconsciously, for what parent would knowingly impede his or her child's educational progress or contribute to his learning difficulty?

Yet this is often the case. The fulcrum of intellectual performance is very often considered to be the ability to read. It follows, therefore, that parents, who want the most for their children will push their children to read, read, and then read some more.

> Too many parents feel their children must learn to read by the middle of their first year in school. These pressures from parents may create more visual problems than will be outweighed by the fact that the child can recognize the words printed in the readers [Getman, 1962, p. 19].

These parents have unconsciously contributed to their child's future learning difficulties.

But most parents want to help. They have always wanted to help but, generally, have felt inadequate to the task. They have considered the schools to be the private domains of "the teachers" which the children "attend" five days a week and usually undergo some metamorphosis to emerge years later as an educated human being.

Although this may be an exaggeration, it may lie closer to the truth than to the fallacy. When did parents begin to emerge as the much needed partner of education? This seems impossible to pinpoint, but one stage of their emancipation was the assurance that parents were not the sole cause of mental deficiency. According to Lewis, Strauss, and Lehtinen (1960, p. vii):

> A far-flung effect of the reorientation of thinking which followed was to free the normal parents of mentally retarded children from shame and guilt and enable them to bring constructive energies to the solutions of the problems of their children.

The Association for Children with Learning Disabilities (A.C.L.D.) is the leading illustration of how parents have combined their energies to provide for these children. The Association for Children with Learning Disabilities has been in the vanguard for improved education and public recognition of the problems that confront these children. Branches of this organization can be found in almost every state and it became an international organization in 1952.

Knowledge about children was more widespread and generally, parents were interested enough to aid and supplement the educational field to provide needed activities. Also, books (Getman, 1962; Lewis, Strauss and Lehtinen, 1960; Siegel, 1961) were beginning to be written in the language of the lay person so that parents could become better informed.

The education and involvement of parents plays a vital role in the area of learning difficulties. Treatment of these children with learning difficulties is a major concern, but equally so is the prevention; in this area parents are indispensable. An example of how parents can help prevent learning difficulties through understanding of early symptoms can be seen in a list of signs suggestive of deafness in infants and young children (Gesell and Amatruda, 1947, p. 278). To be forewarned is to be forearmed, as the saying goes, and in the case of learning difficulties nothing could be more true.

The parent of the emotionally disturbed child also feels more assured when he knows that help is there and that the child will not be relegated to the trash heap of social misfits. Often this type of child is emotionally disturbed because of some deeper rooted learning problem.

As regards the emotionally disturbed child, there are often multiple benefits derived from parent involvement.

There are obvious advantages in having a child in his own home while he is attending school. . . . The restoration of harmony and understanding between parents and child is a major purpose of treatment. Treatment of him and of his parents can go hand in hand and reduce the danger of conflict being set up between different standards of the home and school environments [Peter, 1965, p. 157].

These are only a few examples of how parents in the field of learning difficulties are aided and can contribute to the well-being of these children. The list goes on including the partially-sighted child, the speech-handicapped child and others (Kirk, 1962).

Now let us turn our attention toward what efforts are being made to provide for these children.

PRESENT DAY ATTEMPTS TO ADVANCE

Authorities in education are now reassessing their outlooks on the child with learning difficulties. One concept being severely questioned is that of readiness (Davis, 1948; Havighurst, 1951; Olson, 1959; Tyler, 1948-1949). Learning is a constant activity and some of the most productive years are being ignored by keeping a child out of school until he is five. The concept of preschool and kindergarten as play schools rather than as learning centers is being drastically overhauled. Also, some children with learning difficulties never achieve "readiness" as the term is most often defined, for the simple reason that they never learn the basic fundamentals.

The severely handicapped child is easily identified and is soon placed in a special class. But what of the child who does not fit in any set category? Here, the programs for learning difficulties are offering new hope. These programs are not only a desired innovation in education, but an imperative one. The regular classroom teacher must be relieved of the child with certain learning difficulties that the teacher is not equipped to handle, and of the criticism so often directed toward the teacher for not providing the proper educational atmosphere for all his charges.

One example of a student who might have a learning difficulty is the brain-injured child and since, according to Lewis, Strauss and Lehtinen (1960, p. 127), the normative educational approach does not recognize the brain-injured child as a special case in education, "parents cannot expect the teacher to recognize the specifics of the problem." These children range from above average to borderline cases and meet almost any criteria mentioned for the normal child. Also, the behavior problems one hears about from so many teachers may refer to the same child who is not being provided for in the general curriculum. But, according to Freidus (1957, p. 6),

> In the field of education, techniques for perceptual training and for training in organization of behavior are being developed. Unfortunately, opportunities for a brain-injured child to receive the special training that he requires are still far too rare.

Attempts have been made to provide classes in the public schools to accommodate these children. In 1955, due to the efforts of concerned parents, the first such public school class in New York was established. A second has since been established but we are still far from having adequate provision. The foundation for these classes was laid in 1949, when the Joliet School District, Joliet, Illinois, launched an experimental program to teach brain-injured children. This experiment was a milestone in that it showed what could be done.

At present, the only alternatives for parents of severely brain-injured children are usually expensive private schools. There are excellent schools, as exemplified by the Cove Schools in Racine, Wisconsin, and Evanston, Illinois, but even these schools do not begin to meet the needs of modern education.

> Early in life, the brain-injured child shows signs of a handicap which cripples him severely, whether or not his muscles are affected. Unless he is treated as a special case, his education is not likely to be successful in enabling him to compensate for his handicap. The nature of his deviation from normal society requires a method which takes his disability into account.
>
> When this is recognized by parents and teachers, the child has an even chance to fulfill himself [Lewis, Strauss and Lehtinen, 1951, p. 106].

Where is this method? In what guise will it appear?

A PROGNOSIS

Where are we going? In this chapter, only a few of the cases to be considered have been treated. These cases, however, may illustrate the pressing need for a special program that can meet the needs of the child with learning difficulties, but which, because of his normal or near-normal intelligence, has not been provided.

Do we need a program for the emotionally disturbed? Besides the obvious considerations of the mental health of the unprepared teacher who must cope with him and the cost to the education of the other students because of the time spent treating him, the answer must be an enthusiastic Yes.

> A long range study of 45,000 California school children found 1200 emotionally handicapped. Half were placed in special programs, and half in regular classrooms. The results indicated the superiority of special programs and the inadequacy of providing only mental-health consultations for disturbed children in regular classrooms [Bower, 1961, in Peter, 1965, p. 152].

Mental health happens to be the number one health problem in the United States. When teachers are treating this learning difficulty they may, in actuality, be preventing a national problem.

The "Other Child" needs this program. He is that child who is minimally brain-injured and does not fit into any of the special programs now available in our public schools.

According to Freidus (1957, p. 7),

> To date, no reliable statistical data are available regarding the number of brain-injured children in the general population. . . .
> It is encouraging to note that diagnostic techniques are being perfected so that it is becoming possible to recognize and help such children in their pre-school years when the most significant therapeutic progress can be made.

This program shall also fit the *interim child,* as he shall be called here. He is the minimally multihandicapped child, who will probably comprise the greatest enrollment in classes for children with learning difficulties. He may be brain-injured, he may not be able to read, he might be emotionally disturbed, or lack prowess in athletics. In most school districts there are no special classes for him, but there is very little future also. As he grows older, he often grows more frustrated. He must be given full and equal opportunity in our public schools—and not in the regular classroom.

It was noted earlier in this chapter that the gifted child has been notoriously neglected. This sad condition is being remedied somewhat with our new focus on the gifted, but what of the *underachieving* gifted child? He most certainly needs help with his learning difficulty, if it is nothing more than just poor study habits. According to Kirk (1962, p. 72):

> It would appear that if schools are going to help underachieving bright children a more drastic shift in emphasis will have to be made. This may include:
>
> 1. Identifying underachieving gifted children during the early years in school.
> 2. Assigning tutors to be supportive and to motivate the children through success in academic achievement. This can be done more readily on a one-to-one basis than in a regular classroom situation.
> 3. Counseling with the parents concerning the problems of the child and attempting to produce better home relations.
> 4. Rewarding the child by praise and recognition in school for efforts and achievement in academic work.
> 5. Organizing small special classes for the underachieving gifted children, with special teachers, preferably male if the preponderance of such children are mostly boys.

These five points are all basic to the concept of a program for individuals with learning difficulties.

Remediation for children with severe learning difficulties may be removed from the general curriculum and, instead, be welded into a program for children with learning difficulties. Rather than a spotty, hazardous, catch-as-catch-can approach, remediation should be inaugurated by specialists who, after testing, identifying and verifying that remedial work is indeed necessary, shall proceed to aid the child and then allow him to return to the regular classroom.

A specific area of physical education may be incorporated into this program for those children who lack necessary motor and/or perceptual skills. This class should be based upon sound principles of improvement of learning through the motor, visual and perceptual areas as exemplified by Delacato (1963), Kephart (1960), Roach and Kephart (1966), and others.

Provision will have to be made for the child who possesses a learning difficulty *and* a learning disability. To circumvent his disability and ameliorate his learning difficulty, a classroom may be provided to teach the child through nonreading techinques, if the disability happens to be one of reading. This would include tapes, filmstrips, kinesthetic (role-playing) approaches to learning and project-based activities, i.e., building models, drawing and illustrating, and field trips. The opportunities are endless and *initially* rather expensive, but the final product could be a child equipped to take his place in the community as a productive, contributing member.

Education must recognize this child with a learning difficulty, not only for education's sake, but for the sake of the child. Getman (1962, p. 10) stated,

> If a child, for some environmental, genetic or traumatic reason, does not fit into the acceptable social patterns (which have been too greatly overemphasized in our culture), then this child has been labeled as defective, deficient or delinquent without enough consideration of his membership in the human race.

A new emphasis will be placed on the child during his preschool years. It is here that many later learning difficulties can be nipped in the bud. The child may have to be retained in kindergarten because he possesses neither the necessary academic skills nor the emotional stability to enter first grade. It is much easier on the child and the school to retain a child at this level, than in the sixth, seventh or eighth grade when much of the damage has already taken place and a social stigma attached to retention.

Because of the complexity of programs for children with learning difficulties, new spheres of authority will need to be drawn. Since the administration of such a program is vital to its success, the teacher in charge will have to possess a certain degree of autonomy. This will mean that the principals and/or superintendents of districts will serve slightly different functions than in the past. This does *not* mean that they will surrender to the new programs, but rather will be an integral part of these programs in those areas in which they are most proficient. This phase will be discussed in Chapter 8.

The programs for children with learning difficulties will have to be sold to boards of education, administrations, other special teachers and communities. For this reason, a teacher in this area should be knowledgeable about public relations, news releases, presentations before groups and, above all, have the ability to work with other personnel. These qualities, which are often expected of the regular classroom teacher but are just as often found lacking, play an important role in the success of a program for children with learning difficulties.

Historically, the needs of society have been given to the schools to solve, i.e., if greater scientific skills were needed, the schools were pushed to produce, if business felt a void in their managerial ranks, funds were found to finance new educational programs. In our time, when crime seems to be on the upswing and society cannot understand these sudden outbursts of youth, schools will be expected to provide the solution in conjunction with the family. Programs in learning difficulties, while they may never be the wonder drug or cure-all, may be the safety valve in providing self-assessments in the borderline cases of our school children, and in turn, of our general school population.

CHAPTER 5

Educational Therapy for Individuals with Reading Difficulties

EDUCATIONAL THERAPY has been defined by Ashlock and Stephen (1966, pp. 3-4) as

> The treatment of learning disorders through the application of educational and psychological principles of learning and adjustment. Such treatment is usually used as a prelude to, or in conjunction with, specialized educational techniques and materials employed to diminish the discrepancy between the learner's academic potential and level of attainment.

Educational therapy includes describing the child's learning problem, helping him understand it, and helping him plan and move successfully into a specialized reading program.

DESCRIBING THE PROBLEM

Considering Psychophysiological Factors

In this book, psychophysiological approaches are those of a general, or overall, nature as distinguished from more narrow, perceptual-motor approaches. Usually, the psychophysiological approaches require that the child use all of his body or a major portion of it. The general theory is that certain physical movements will improve the functioning of the central nervous system. If this functioning is improved, it is assumed that reading performance will then improve or remedial instruction will be made easier.

Children who might benefit from a psychophysiological approach may include those who have the following types of problems:

1. *General lack of motor coordination* such as poor balance,

clumsiness, illegible handwriting, poor eye-hand coordination, left-right confusion, etc.

2. *More specific inadequacies in motor coordination* such as difficulties with cutting, coloring, pasting, and copying; reversals in reading, writing, and spelling; poor sense of direction; difficulty in catching things thrown to him; lack of fluency in reading, etc.

3. *Speech difficulties* such as mispronunciation of words usually pronounced correctly by peers, quite rapid and/or slurred speech, omissions of words, difficulty in expressing himself, etc.

4. *Behavioral inadequacies* such as confusion in following directions, hyperactivity, carelessness, distractibility, short attention span, tendencies to push, shove, and generally make a nuisance of himself, etc.

Psychophysiological approaches vary according to the theoretical assumptions of the originator of the approach. Three approaches are described here with attention drawn to some of their distinguishing characteristics.

Delacato

Delacato and his associates at the Institutes for the Development of Human Potential have developed a rigid, highly specific type of treatment for neurologically impaired or neurologically underdeveloped children. The diagnosis and treatment of such children are described in Delacato's books, *The Treatment and Prevention of Reading Problems* and *The Diagnosis and Treatment of Speech and Reading Problems.*" "The Ontogeny of Reading Problems" by Delacato can be obtained in reprint form from the Institutes. This article gives a rather concise summary of the theory underlying this approach. *The Doman-Delacato Developmental Mobility Scale* and *The Doman-Delacato-Doman Developmental Language Scale* help to further explain this program.

The Delacato approach, it must be kept in mind, is based upon a still unproven theory. The theory applies to a rather specific group of children. Some rather dramatic results have been shown in individual instances. Conclusive research findings concerning the approach are still lacking.

To decide whether or not a child may need some of the Delacato work described previously, the remedial teacher may use the diagnostic procedures described in either of Delacato's books (1959; 1963).

A much more simplified procedure can be found in *A Handbook of Information on Carl H. Delacato's Neurological Approach to Reading Instruction* prepared by a group of reading specialists and available from the Archdiocesian Reading Service, Catholic Charities, 126 North Desplaines, Chicago, Illinois, 60606.

Kephart

The keystone of Kephart's approach is *flexibility*. The training procedures are aimed at making the student facile and pliant in an environment which makes ever increasing, ever changing, demands. There is nothing narrow or rigid about Kephart's approach. Once the basic theory is understood, the teacher may try any type of procedure which appears to be directed toward achieving the goal toward which the teacher and student are working. As Kephart has said in his speaking engagements, "If it works, it's right."

Kephart has found through years of experience and research that children who have learning problems often have problems with basic motor skills. He has constructed a theory characterized by its common sense, down-to-earth basis.

Kephart's work with youngsters at the Achievement Center for Children on the Purdue University campus is constantly resulting in changes and improvements in Kephart's ideas. The noncult atmosphere has stimulated a number of significant research studies. For the reader who is interested in learning more about this interesting research, Dunsing's "An Annotated Bibliography of Research and Theory Related to the Achievement Center for Children," available from the center, is recommended.

Kephart's diagnostic procedures are described in his book *The Slow Learner in the Classroom*. His "Perceptual Survey

Rating Scale" has now been standardized, and is called the *Purdue Perceptual-Motor Survey* (Roach and Kephart, 1966).

Frostig

Basic to Frostig's visual perception training program (Frostig and Horne, 1944; Frostig, 1961; Frostig, Lefever, and Whittlesey, 1961; Frostig, Maslow, Lefever and Whittlesey, 1963a; Frostig, Maslow, Lefever, and Whittlesey, 1963b) is a plan for motor facilitation. Some of the topics in this plan are position in space, spatial relationships, perceptual constancy, visual-motor coordination, and figure-ground perception.

Frostig's diagnostic procedures are described in her *Administration and Scoring Manual for the Marianne Frostig Developmental Test of Visual Perception* (Frostig, Lefever, and Whittlesey, 1964).

Considering Sensory Acuity

It is most important that screening for sensory defects be made on all individuals with learning difficulties. One set of screening devices that can be used by the teacher are the *Keystone Visual Survey Tests* (Keystone View Company, 1933-1958). Although it is necessary to purchase an instrument, the Telebinocular, for use in making this survey, it is well worth the investment. The screening involves both near and far point vision. A number of other possible visual anomalies can be tested for. If the child fails two screenings, he should be referred to a medical specialist for a thorough examination.

For years the Snellen charts have been used to test far point vision. These can be obtained from the National Society for the Prevention of Blindness, 1790 Broadway, New York, New York, 10019. Now, near point vision can be tested by the classroom teacher through the use of the *Good-Lite Reading Cards for Adults and Children* available from the Good-Lite Company, 7426 West Madison Street, Forest Park, Illinois, 60130.

Each remedial reader should have an individual audiometric examination. When some children have even slight hearing losses at certain frequencies this can explain difficulties in learning phonics.

Considering Perception

It is becoming realized that perceptual difficulties are at least partially responsible for many of children's learning problems.

Marianne Frostig Developmental Test of Visual Perception (Frostig, 1961)

This perceptual test for preschool to grade four (and above if the child seems to be severely perceptually disturbed) is a good device for partially diagnosing the perceptual difficulties of children. Separate scores can be obtained for eye-motor coordination, figure-ground perception, constancy of shape, position in space, and spatial relationships. The test is particularly useful to the reading teacher because an extensive training program has been developed for the correction of the defects found during the test administration (Frostig and Horne, 1964).

Stanford-Binet Intelligence Scale (Terman and Merrill, 1960)

Some of the sections of this intelligence test appear to yield information concerning perception. But since performance on individual sections of the Binet is usually not evaluated separately, the examiner should be asked prior to the testing to be on the lookout for possible perceptual difficulties. Some items which seem to involve perception are the following:

Three-Hole Form Board—year II—visual
Repeating 2 Digits—year II-6—auditory
Obeying Simple Commands—year II-6—auditory
Three-Hole Form Board: Rotated—year II-6—visual
Block Building: Bridge—year III—visual
Copying A Circle—year III—visual
Drawing a Verticle Line—year III—visual
Repeating 3 Digits—year III—auditory
Comparison of Balls—year III-6—visual
Patience: Pictures—year III-6—visual
Discrimination of Animal Pictures—year III-6—visual
Comparison of Sticks—year III-6—visual
Discrimination of Forms—year IV—visual
Memory for Sentences I—year IV—auditory

Aesthetic Comparison—year IV-6—visual
Pictorial Similarities and Differences I—year IV-6—visual
Three Commissions—year IV-6—auditory
Picture Completion: Man—year V—visual
Paper Folding: Triangle—year V—visual
Copying a Square—year V—visual
Pictorial Similarities and Differences II—year V—visual
Patience: Rectangles—year V—visual
Knot—year V—visual
Mutilated Pictures—year V—visual
Copying a Diamond—year VII—visual
Repeating 5 Digits—year VII—auditory
Repeating 3 Digits Reversed—year VII—auditory
Paper Cutting—year IX—visual
Memory For Designs—year IX—visual
Rhymes: New Form—year IX—auditory
Repeating 4 Digits Reversed—year IX—auditory
Rhymes: Old Form—year IX—auditory
Repeating 6 Digits—year X—auditory
Memory for Designs I—year XI—visual
Memory for Sentences II—year XI—auditory
Repeating 5 Digits Reversed—year XII—auditory
Memory for Designs II—year XII—visual
Memory for Sentences III—year XIII—auditory
Copying a Bead Chain From Memory—year XIII—visual
Paper Cutting—year XIII—visual
Binet Paper Cutting—Average adult—visual
Repeating 6 Digits Reversed—Superior adult I—auditory

Wechsler Intelligence Scale for Children (Wechsler, 1949)

Parts of the WISC also appear to measure certain aspects of perception.

DIGIT SPAN. The child is asked to repeat series of digits forward and backward. The test appears to measure both auditory perception and auditory memory.

BLOCK DESIGN. In this test, the child is called upon to reproduce a block design or a picture of a block design. The reproduction is made with colored blocks. In Ashlock's study (1963) it was found that there was a +.39 correlation between the block design subtest and reading performance for ninety primary grade children.

OBJECT ASSEMBLY. The child puts together four puzzles.

The test may measure visual perception, reasoning, familiarity with one's environment, manual dexterity, and perceptual speed. Ashlock (1963) found a +.25 correlation between this test and the reading skill of ninety primary grade children.

CODING. The child must perceive, learn, and use a visual code under time pressure. Visual perception, associative ability, and manual dexterity may be involved in the performance of this test. Ashlock (1963) found a +.28 correlation between this test and the reading skill of ninety primary grade children.

Wechsler Adult Intelligence Scale (Wechsler, 1955)

For the individual who may have a perceptual problem and who is sixteen years of age and over, certain subtests of the WAIS may be of value in the description of the learning problem.

DIGIT SPAN. The subject must repeat a series of digits forward and backward. The test appears to measure both auditory perception and auditory memory.

DIGIT SYMBOL. The subject must perceive, learn and use a visual code under time pressure. Visual perception, associative ability, and manual dexterity may be involved in performing this test.

BLOCK DESIGN. In this test, the subject is called upon to reproduce a block design or a picture of a block design. The reproduction is made with colored blocks. Visual perception and manual dexterity may be measured in this test.

OBJECT ASSEMBLY. The subject puts together four puzzles. The test may measure visual perception, reasoning, familiarity with one's environment, manual dexterity, and perceptual speed.

Detroit Tests of Learning Aptitude (Baker and Leland, 1958)

The sections useful in evaluating auditory perception are Auditory Attention Span for Unrelated Words, and Auditory Attention Span for Related Syllables. The sections useful in evaluating visual perception are Visual Attention Span for Objects, Memory for Designs, and Visual Attention Span for Letters.

Auditory Discrimination Test (Wepman, 1958)

Two similar words are pronounced by the examiner. The child must judge whether he has heard the same word twice, or two different words. Two forms of the test are available. This test is basically for children in the primary grades.

Perceptual Forms (Lowder, 1956)

The perceptual form program is one developed by Robert Glenn Lowder in connection with his doctoral work at Purdue. This program is designed to be used in testing the visual perception of youngsters in the primary grades. Like the Frostig materials, there is available a training program for the remediation of visual perceptual difficulties in young children. A unique feature of the program is that there are materials for helping parents and their children at home. Complete information about these diagnostic materials and training programs can be obtained by writing to Winter Haven Lions Publications Committee, P. O. Box 1405, Winter Haven, Florida, 33880.

If it seems that a child might have to be taught through the tactile-kinesthetic method, it is necessary to have some idea of how good the youngster's tactile-kinesthetic perception and memory are. Benton (1955; 1959), Benton, Hutcheon, and Seymor (1951), and Benton and Schultz (1949) have described how to do this type of testing.

Some informal methods for evaluating the tactile-kinesthetic perception of children are the following:

1. a. Have the child tell you which is his thumb, second finger, etc., with his eyes open.
   b. Have him close his eyes and let the examiner touch different fingers with a pencil.
   c. Have the youngster tell the examiner which finger has been touched.
2. a. Show the child letter forms and lay aside the letters he recognizes.
   b. Trace each recognized letter on the youngster's back and see if he can still recognize it.

3. a. Repeat step 2a.

   b. Take the child's arm and trace the recognized letters in the air and see if he can still recognize them.

4. a. Repeat step 2a.

   b. Take the child's hand and trace the recognized letters on a desk top and see if he can recognize them.

5. a. Repeat step 2a.

   b. Divide the unknown letters into two groups.

   c. Cut half of them out of sandpaper, and write the others on paper.

   d. Teach the child the letters, showing him those written on paper and having him trace the sandpaper ones. Observe how long it takes him to learn each group and how well he remembers them.

If the child does well on No. 1, this is some indication that he has adequate body image skills to make some type of tactile-kinesthetic training at least initially successful. If the youngster can recognize known letters when traced on his back as in No. 2, this finding tends to reinforce the results of test No. 1 concerning body image. Tests Nos. 3 and 4 are simply other tests of body image based upon the use of different sensory modalities. Test No. 5 involves the use of two approaches (letters written on paper and sandpaper letters) to teaching unknown words. The use of test No. 5 allows the teacher to make a comparison of the child's ability to learn and remember symbols taught by the visual and tactile-kinesthetic methods.

CONSIDERING INTELLIGENCE

To begin with, it is important that both the teacher and the student obtain an idea of how intelligent the youngster is. Just as it is unfair to expect too much of a child, it is equally damaging to expect too little.

It is not valid to administer to a remedial reader an intelligence test which requires reading. If this is done, the child receives a low score because he cannot handle the reading material, not because he is lacking in intelligence.

These are some good intelligence tests for students who have reading problems:

Wechsler Intelligence Scale for Children (Wechsler, 1949)

This individual intelligence test must be administered by a qaulified psychological examiner. It is for children aged five through fifteen. A verbal IQ, a performance IQ, and a full-scale IQ can be obtained. An examination of the scores earned on the various subtests gives an idea of the structure of the child's intellect as measured by this test. The subtests and what they appear to test (in this author's opinion) are given here.

GENERAL INFORMATION. A test of how much the child has learned through just living in his environment.

GENERAL COMPREHENSION. A test of "horse sense" and of a sense of personal responsibility.

ARITHMETIC. A test of ability to do arithmetical reasoning under time pressure.

SIMILARITIES. A test of similarities and/or analogies. This subtest appears to be a test of abstract reasoning.

VOCABULARY. A nonreading test of word knowledge. This type of skill would appear to be of importance in the youngster's ability to understand the reading material that he may be taught in the future.

DIGIT SPAN. The administration of this test is optional for the examiner. When requesting that the WISC be given, the special teacher should ask that the Digit Span subtest be given. If this subtest measures auditory attention span and immediate recall, the score should be meaningful to the remedial teacher—especially in the area of phonic instruction.

The preceding WISC subtests make up the Verbal Scale. The following subtests make up the Performance Scale.

PICTURE COMPLETION. A test of knowledge of the environment and of visual perception. If the child cannot say the answer, the examiner should tell the student to point to the missing part of each picture. But the examiner should note that the child cannot verbalize some of his responses. This fact may point up a need for further testing in the area of language development. This subtest is timed.

PICTURE ARRANGEMENT. A test of social intelligence in which the child is required to arrange a set of pictures to tell a sensible story. When the story layout is finished, it looks somewhat like a comic strip.

BLOCK DESIGN. The child uses colored blocks to copy geometric designs. Poor performance on this test is sometimes interpreted as a possible sign of neurological impairment and/or malfunction.

OBJECT ASSEMBLY. The child puts together the parts of four puzzles.

CODING. The child has to make associations between numbers and geometric symbols. The associations are recorded through the use of paper and pencil. This is sometimes thought of as a test of associative memory—involving visual perception and motor skill. This may be true at the very early age levels, but this may be primarily a test of motor ability.

MAZES. Mazes is based upon the childhood game of getting out of a maze without getting lost in a blind alley. In this optional subtest of the WISC, Mazes is a pencil and paper operation. Although highly prized by British psychologists, this type of test is not too often used in the United States. Superficially, this is a test of abstract reasoning based upon spatial relations.

Wechsler Adult Intelligence Scale (Wechsler, 1955)

This is the adult version of the Wechsler Intelligence Scale for Children. It is for subjects aged sixteen through adulthood. The rationale is basically the same as for the WISC. The Coding of the WISC becomes, in essence, the Digit Symbol of the WAIS. There are six verbal subtests: Information, Comprehension, Arithmetic, Similarities, Digit Span, and Vocabulary. There are five performance subtests: Digit Symbol, Picture Completion, Block Design, Picture Arrangement, and Object Assembly. There are no optional subtests on the WAIS.

Wechsler Preschool and Primary School of Intelligence (Wechsler, 1966)

The WPPSI, in general, is constructed along the principles used in developing the other Wechsler tests. The WPPSI is for children aged four to six and one half years. As with the other Wechsler tests, a verbal IQ, a performance IQ, and a full-scale IQ can be obtained. The verbal tests include Information, Vocabulary, Similarities, Comprehension, Arithmetic, and Sentences (optional). The performance tests include Animal House, Picture Completion, Mazes, Geometric Design, and Block Design. Because of the newness of the test, many administrations of it will have to be done by various workers in the field before a determination of its usefulness with children who may develop reading difficulties can be made.

Stanford-Binet Intelligence Scale (Terman and Merrill, 1960)

This individual intelligence test might best be used with preschool children and children in the primary grades. It must be administered by a person who has training in psychological testing. One disadvantage of the test is that it is a test of global intelligence and a breakdown of different types of intellectual functioning cannot usually be done except by a very skilled psychological examiner *who has a good background in education.* In everyday use, the S-B appears to be of little practical diagnostic value.

Detroit Tests of Learning Aptitude (Baker and Leland, 1958)

Although this is an individual test of intelligence, it can be administered by the special teacher or educational therapist who may have limited training in individual psychological testing. This test can be used at the preschool level through adulthood. There is some flexibility in choosing which subtests are to be administered to an individual. The DTLA is recommended as a good intelligence test for poor readers and for children who have other learning problems. The subtest titles, in the main, explain themselves, except where explanatory remarks in parenthesis have been added:

1. Pictorial Absurdities
2. Verbal Absurdities
3. Pictorial Opposites
4. Verbal Opposites
5. Motor Speed (and motor coordination)

6. Auditory Attention Span for Unrelated Words (simple score and weighted score can give evidence of auditory memory of unsequential and sequential orders)
7. Oral Commissions (oral directions)
8. Social Adjustment A
9. Visual Attention Span for Objects (same as No. 6, except this test relates to the visual factor)
10. Orientation (knowledge of self in space)
11. Free Association (verbal fluency)
12. Designs (excellent test for visual perception)
13. Auditory Attention Span for Related Syllables (involves cognition)
14. Number Ability
15. Social Adjustment B
16. Visual Attention Span for Letters (excellent test of visual perception)
17. Disarranged Pictures
18. Oral Directions
19. Likenesses and Differences (abstract reasoning)

Considering Language

While language development is of central importance to the teacher of children with learning difficulties, *speech* should usually be left to a trained speech therapist.

Probably the most valuable test of language development is the observation of the teacher who has had wide experience with children. If a more structured observation of language development in the young child is desired, the *Illinois Test of Psycholinguistic Abilities* (McCarthy and Kirk, 1961) can be administered. If the ITPA is given, the pattern of scores is probably of more value to the teacher than the scores themselves.

Considering Personality

When the problem learner is suspected of having very severe emotional problems, he should be referred to a clinical psychologist for an evaluation. Sometimes disturbed remedial readers should be given therapy before attempting remedial work. At other times, the two can be carried on concurrently. It is rare that remedial reading instruction in itself will get a child over a *severe* emotional problem.

For the special teacher, one of the better tests of personality is the *California Test of Personality* (Thorpe, Clark, and Tiegs, 1953). There are forms available for individuals in the early grades and on into adulthood. As with other tests of this type, they should be read to the individual who has a reading problem. Some of the factors covered in the CTP are self-reliance, sense of personal worth, sense of personal freedom, feeling of belonging, freedom from withdrawal tendencies, freedom from nervous symptoms, total personal adjustment, social standards, social skills, freedom from antisocial tendencies, family relations, school relations or occupational relations, community relations, total social adjustment, and total adjustment. The scores themselves are probably not as important as the skill the teacher uses in questioning the individual about responses that he has made.

The teacher interested in going into personality testing in more depth is referred to *The Sixth Mental Measurements Yearbook* (Buros, 1965) and *Tests in Print* (Buros, 1961). A good coverage of identification of emotional problems can be found in *The Early Identification of Emotionally Handicapped Children in School* (Bower, 1960).

Actually, if the teacher is dealing with adjustment problems rather than severe emotional problems (which are not in his province anyway) he may do better to stick to interview techniques rather than make excessive use of personality tests. As Phillips, Wiener, and Haring (1960) have noted, it is not always purposeful for the teacher to know first causes. As these authors have stated, the knowledge of first causes of the problem may "lead nowhere for classroom purposes." What the teacher needs to do is to formulate a learning plan in which the child can cope with the adjustment problems that he is experiencing at this time.

Considering Reading Performance

The next step in the educational therapeutic treatment of

the child is an evaluation of reading performance. Some reading tests of use in this area are described:

Tests of General Reading Performance

Gates-MacGinitie Reading Tests, Primary A (Gates and MacGinitie, 1965): There are two alternate forms of this test of vocabulary and comprehension for first grade.

Gates-MacGinitie Reading Tests, Primary B (Gates and MacGinitie, 1965): The same as the preceding, but for grade two.

Gates-MacGinitie Reading Tests, Primary C (Gates and MacGinitie, 1965): The same as the preceding, but for grade three.

Gates-MacGinitie Reading Tests, Primary CS (Gates and MacGinitie, 1965): A supplementary test for the Primary C, for grades 2.5 and three; three alternate forms are available.

Gates-MacGinitie Reading Tests, Survey D (Gates and MacGinitie, 1965): There are three alternate forms of this test of speed, vocabulary, and comprehension for grades four through six.

Gates-MacGinitie Reading Tests, Survey E (Gates and MacGinitie, 1965): There are three alternate forms of this test of speed, vocabulary, and comprehension for grades seven through nine.

Gates-MacGinitie Reading Tests, Survey F (Gates and MacGinitie, in preparation): The same as the preceding, but for grades ten through twelve.

Sequential Tests of Educational Progress: Reading (Cooperative Test Division, 1956-1963): The STEP comes in four levels for grades four through six, seven through nine, ten through twelve, and thirteen through fourteen. Types of reading material included are fiction, poetry, rhymes, plays, letters, directions for doing something, announcements, articles of opinion, explanations, and information. The tests were designed to measure skill in five areas of reading: ability to recall ideas, ability to translate ideas and make inferences, ability to analyze the intent of the author, ability to analyze presentation, and ability to constructively criticize.

Davis Reading Test (Davis and Davis, 1956-1962): This·
is a well constructed and well standardized test of level and
speed comprehension. *Series 1* is for individuals in grades eleven
through thirteen. *Series 2* is for students in grades eight into
eleven. There are four alternate forms for each series.

*The Nelson-Denny Reading Test: Vocabulary-Comprehen-
sion-Rate* (Nelson, Denny, and Brown, 1929-1960): Four scores
can be obtained from the administration of this test: vocabulary,
comprehension, total, and rate. The test is limited by its range,
being for grades nine through sixteen and for adults. The Nelson-Denny however, is one of the few good tests which we have
for evaluating the general reading performance of this age range.

Diagnostic Reading Tests

Diagnostic Reading Tests (Committee on Diagnostic Reading Tests, 1947-1963): These tests are designed to test general
reading proficiency and a number of specific reading skills in
students from kindergarten through grade thirteen. The types
of skills included in the various tests differ with different grades
and grade groupings. The quality of the tests varies with different grade levels. The teacher of youngsters with learning
difficulties is advised to examine an appropriate specimen set
before ordering tests for an individual or a group. Certain levels
are appropriate for our children and some are not. Current evaluation of the tests as a whole is difficult because of the extensive
amount of research which is being conducted relative to the
tests at the time of this printing.

Roswell-Chall Auditory Blending Test (Roswell and Chall,
1963): This informal inventory was designed to test the student's ability to blend sounds into whole words. The test is administered individually and is for grades one through four.

*Roswell-Chall Diagnostic Reading Test of Word Analysis
Skills* (Roswell and Chall, 1956-1959): There are two forms of
this test to be used in grades two through six. This test too, is
more of an informal inventory than a diagnostic test. Word
analysis skills included in the test are consonants, consonant
combinations, short vowels, silent *e* rule, vowel combinations,
and syllabication. The test is seriously limited in scope, but may

provide the experienced teacher with a rough idea of the state of the youngster's word analysis skills.

Gates-McKillop Reading Diagnostic Tests (Gates and Mc-Killop, 1962): This individual test is to be used in making a detailed analysis of a child's reading problem. The oral reading selection seems to be rather poor. The test is good when the teacher is working with very small numbers of youngsters. This test can be used in grades two through six.

Silent Reading Diagnostic Tests: The Developmental Reading Tests (Bond, Clymer, and Hoyt, 1955): These tests are for youngsters in grades three through eight. There is only one form of the test. It is designed for group use. These tests consist of the following sections: Recognition of Words in Isolation, Recognition of Words in Context, Recognition of Reversible Words in Context, Locating Elements, Syllabication, Locating the Word, Word Elements, Beginning Sounds, Rhyming Sounds, Letter Sounds and Word Synthesis. Twenty scores can be obtained: six word recognition pattern scores, four error analysis scores, nine word recognition techniques scores, and word synthesis.

California Phonics Survey (Brown and Cottrell, 1956-1963): This phonics survey is for grades seven through twelve and college. Form 2 yields only a total score. Form 1 yields nine error scores: long-short vowel confusion, other vowel confusion, consonants-confusion with blends and digraphs, consonant-vowel reversals, configuration, endings, negatives-opposites-sight words, rigidity, and a total score. One advantage of this test is that it can be administered by the use of a tape recording, thus eliminating differences of pronunciation by different examiners. Although no data on the reliability of subscores is given, this may not be a serious drawback as far as actual teaching is concerned.

Diagnostic Reading Scales (Spache, 1963a): This test is for youngsters in grades one through eight and for individuals with reading difficulties in grades nine through twelve. Aspects of reading which this test purports to measure are word recognition, oral reading, silent reading, rate of silent reading (optional), potential level (auditory comprehension), consonant sounds, vowel sounds, consonant blends, common syllables, blending, and letter sounds.

The user should be cautioned about the advisability of using an auditory comprehension test to measure potential reading level. There is one form of this test and it is to be administered individually.

Oral Reading Tests

one of the best!

Gilmore Oral Reading Paragraphs (Gilmore, 1951-1952): This is probably one of the best oral reading tests because the context is sensible and well constructed. Comprehension is checked after each paragraph. A form is provided for the use of the teacher in recording different types of oral reading errors. There are two alternate forms of this test for youngsters in grades one through eight.

Gray Oral Reading Test (Robinson and Gray, 1963): There are four alternate forms of this test for individual administration to students in grades one through sixteen and for adults. This instrument is constructed to test oral reading, rate of reading, and types of errors made. Four questions concerning literal meaning are asked after each passage is read. Mistakes made in oral reading are classified into eight categories: aid on words, gross and partial mispronunciations, omissions, insertions, substitutions, repetitions, and inversions.

THE BUILDUP

As noted by Ashlock and Stephen (1966, p. 45) the buildup, or preparation for remedial instruction is an integral part of educational therapy. The buildup should precede remediation and develop the student's potential for benefiting from remedial instruction.

The Psychophysiological Buildup

The teacher who, through the use of psychophysiological diagnostic procedures discussed previously in this chapter, has discovered individuals who need training in this area may be interested in consulting the following works:

Diagnosis and Treatment of Speech and Reading Problems (Delacato, 1959)

Treatment and Prevention of Reading Problems (Delacato, 1963)

Neurological Organization and Reading (Delacato, 1966)

The Slow Learner in the Classroom (Kephart, 1960)

Aids to Motoric and Perceptual Training (Kephart, 1964)

The Frostig Program for the Development of Visual Perception (Frostig, 1964)

Some Thoughts about Psychophysiological Approaches

BAND WAGON. Since the concept of the psychophysiological approach is still rather new, there is the always present danger that it will become a fad. We must keep in mind that this approach is for children who have certain identifiable problems. In other words, the psychophysiological approach is not meant to be a cure for everything from brain damage to warts.

NOT THROUGH THE BODY ALONE. Just as man does not live by bread alone, it does not seem that a child who has a learning problem can usually be straightened out through use of psychophysiological approach alone.

HAWTHORNE EFFECT. The Hawthorne effect occurs when any special treatment affects a person, not because the treatment is particularly beneficial, but because the person responds to being treated specially. Since the psychophysiological approach is so special, we must keep the possibility of the Hawthorne effect in mind when we try to account for the success of the students being treated with this method.

TRUST IN THE TEACHER. It has been the author's experience that the more the youngster trusts the teacher and respects his professional knowledge, the more likely it is that the student will cooperate and respond successfully. Sometimes one can just see the child relax and literally "put himself into the hands" of a trusted teacher. This is the kind of situation that can produce results regardless of the approach used.

THE EXPLANATION COUNTS. The psychophysiological approach is different and strange to a youngster. If the reasons for using such an approach are not carefully explained to the child, he may worry and imagine that all sorts of things are wrong with him. But if the theory is explained to the student, and if teacher and child embark on the experimental program together, there is a good chance for success.

A *Proposed Program of Physical Skill Building*

We tend to suspect that a generalized program of physical skill development may be as effective as programs which follow some of them are specific theories in this area. While we *at this time* do not subscribe to any particular theory, we lean to some extent toward Kephart's eclectic approach. There is not at present enough experimental evidence (and in particular, not enough longitudinal studies) to support a specialized theoretical approach.

A basic outline such as the following might, with necessary adaptations, be useful in dealing with individuals who may have various types of psychophysiological problems.

BODY IMAGE. Body image consists of knowledge of location of body parts and their relation to each other. This knowledge eventually has to be internalized to the point that the child can use it in terms of abstract, mental concepts. Exercises which might be of help in developing body image are angels-in-the-snow, identification of body parts, and identification of body parts of a partner. Some of the workers in the field who have dealt with body image are Kephart (1960), Harres (1963), Cobb (1958), Gellhorn (1960), Schilder (1964), Allport (1961), Humphrey (1963), Goodenough and Tyler (1959), and Cratty (1967).

MOVEMENT OF THE BODY IN SPACE. It seems to be important that the child learn to handle his body efficiently in space. This skill has two aspects: (a) use of the body in positions other than the stationary upright one and (b) use of the body in different spatial media. Activities which might fit into the first classification are gym scooter activities, crab walk, tumbling, hip walk, running, modified push-ups, the hip lift, picnic table, side-leaning rest, horseback riding, and driving a car. Activities which might be included in the second category include swimming, trampoline, high jump, hurdles, and bar activities. References which might be of use in these areas are Dauer (1962), Burns and Micoleau (1957), and Cratty (1967).

RHYTHM. Rhythm is involved in the performance of a number of synchronized movements either in response to external stimuli or internal rhythmic plans. Activities which might be of value in this area are rhythm band, walking to tempo, marching, skipping, dancing, and movement or motion exploration. Publications of interest in this area are Andrews (1954), Kephart (1960), Evans (1958), Heaton (1959), Hughes (1954), Lunt (1959), Metz (1962), Murray (1953), and Sehon and O'Brien (1951).

DIRECTIONALITY. Directionality consist of the ability to maintain and change direction upon command or desire. Good directionality includes a well-internalized sense of right and left. Training activities in this area might include command marching, relays and variations of relays, square dancing, target skills, and lead-up games. Significant references in this area include Kephart (1960), Dauer (1962), Roach and Kephart (1966), Benton (1959), Belmont and Birch (1963), Leavell and Beck (1959), and Cratty (1967).

POSTURE CONTROL. Posture control pertains to the ability to maintain a certain alignment of body parts over a given period of time. Balance is included in posture control. Some suggestions for training posture control include balance board and balance beam, stork stand, skating, bicycle riding, ballet, gymnastics, and skiing. Some sources in this area are Seashore (1947), Darrow (1959), Phelps, Kipphuth, and Goff, (1956), Davies (1958), Kelley (1949), Lowman and Young (1960), and Cratty (1967).

COORDINATION. Coordination is the ability to use two or more parts of the body in a meaningful pattern. Activities in this area include dancing, batting, throwing, bowling, golf, and most sports with carry-over value. References in this area include Athletic Institute (1951), Halsey and Porter (1958), Larson and Hill (1957), O'Keefe and Aldrich (1959), American Association for Health, Physical Education and Recreation (1960), and Wilkinson (1967).

MINIMUM MUSCULAR EFFICIENCY. Muscular efficiency includes minimum muscular fitness, appropriate range of motion, and proper reflex conditioning. Activities include pretraining skills, adaptive and resistive exercises, command march drill, square dance, catching objects, and "freeze" games. Suggested readings in this area include Kephart (1960), American Association for Health, Physical Education and Recreation (1961), President's Council on Youth Fitness (1961), Dauer (1962), Royal Canadian Air Force (1962), Magoun (1963), Wilkinson (1967), Cureton (1965), Luria (1963), and Cratty (1967).

BODY FLEXIBILITY. Body flexibility pertains to a smooth and facile physiology of motion. Training procedures include warm-up drills and skills, baseball and softball, basketball, football, gymnastics, water sports, and wrestling. Source materials in this area include Kephart (1960), Cureton (1965), Dauer (1962), Berdard (1962), Szypula (1957), Burns and Micoleau (1957), Wilkinson (1967), and Cratty (1967).

FINE MUSCLE CONTROL. Fine muscle control pertains to the coordination of the small muscles involved in handwriting, typing, drawing, painting, etc. Activities in this area might include playing marbles, pick up sticks, ball and jacks, card playing, mumbly peg, Chinese checkers, tiddley-winks, finger painting, clay modeling, paper and pencil games, Frostig materials, Continental Press materials, coloring, cutting, tracing, chalkboard activities, and arts and crafts. Readings in this area might include Frostig (1964), Ashlock and Stephen (1966), Berger (1961), Bell (1960), and the catalogs from companies such as Developmental Learning Materials, Teaching Resources, Childcraft Equipment Company, Continental Press, Creative Playthings, Whitman Publishing Company and Ideal.

OCULAR CONTROL. Ocular control includes adequate coordination of the eyes, correct sighting, and eye-hand coordination. Activities in this area include lacing frame, "following the dots," sighting skills such as shooting a gun and archery, threading a needle, sewing cards, and copying from the chalkboard. Sources relative to this area include Kephart (1960), Roach and Kephart (1966), Getman (1962), Small (1958), Werner and Strauss (1939), Frostig (1964), and Abercrombie, Gardiner, Hanson, Jonckheere, Lindon, Solomon, and Tyson (1964).

The Sensory Acuity Buildup

The sensory acuity buildup is the realm of the visual, auditory, and medical specialists involved. The responsibility of teacher is to refer, see that the referral is carried through, and make note of how the child functions, acuity-wise, after correction has taken place. Possible correction should usually take place before academic remediation is initiated.

The Perceptual Buildup

When perceptual training is indicated through the use of testing procedures described previously in this chapter, the teacher may wish to consult the following sources:

Educational Therapy in the Elementary School (Ashlock and Stephen, 1966)

The Frostig Program for the Development of Visual Perception (Frostig, 1964)

The Slow Learner in the Classroom (Kephart, 1960)

Aids to Motoric and Perceptual Training (Kephart, 1964)

The Montessori Method (Montessori, 1964)

Dr. Montessori's Own Handbook (Montessori, 1965a)

The Montessori Elementary Manual (Montessori, 1965b)

Learning How to Learn (Rambush, 1962)

Psychopathology and Education of the Brain-Injured Child: Vol. I (Strauss and Lehtinen, 1947)

Psychopathology and Education of the Brain-Injured Child: Vol. II (Strauss and Kephart, 1955)

Perception and Cerebral Palsy (Cruickshank, Bice, and Wallen, 1957)

A Teaching Method for Brain-Injured and Hyperactive Children (Cruickshank, *et al*, 1961)

Learning Disabilities, Educational Principles and Practices (Johnson and Myklebust, 1967)

Intelligence

While nothing can be done about a child's hereditary intellectual endowment, it is felt that some help can be given to the child in relation to environmental stimulation and to the facilitation of his intellectual functioning. For the teacher interested in this area, the following readings are suggested:

How to Increase Your Child's Intelligence (Getman, 1962)

Help Your Child Learn How to Learn (Avery and Higgins, 1962)

Success Through Play (Radler and Kephart, 1960)

The Language Buildup

For the teacher of the youngster who has been found to have a language problem, the following references might be of use:

Slow to Talk (Beasley, 1956)

"*Language and Behavior of Children with Unsuspected Brain Injury*" (Clark, 1962)

Speech and Language Therapy with the Brain-Damaged Child (Daley, 1962)

"*Communicative Disorders in Children*" (Harrington, 1962)

Language Disorders in Children (Wood, 1959)

The Personality Buildup

Some of the best results in this area can be obtained by just talking with the youngster. By this, it is not meant that the special reading teacher should use nondirective counseling with the youngster. Most youngsters who have learning problems are nondirected enough already. What they need is some guidance from an understanding adult. Some of the things youngsters may benefit from discussing with teachers are the following:

1. *Why the problem exists.* The youngster usually wants concrete reasons and not vague "pedagogical" explanations. Even at the risk of upsetting the child, knowing the truth may be less threatening than what he is imagining.
2. *Some suggestions as to what the youngster can do to help himself.* It is no favor to a youngster to make him feel that everything depends upon the teacher.
3. *How the youngster feels about the problem.* Even if you have to drag it out of him, it is sometimes a relief for the child to put his feelings about the problem into words.

4. *How he can make contact with his parents about the problem.* Sometimes it is difficult for a youngster and his parents to talk about a school problem. If the teacher can give the child just a push toward working with his parents, a lot of tension can be relieved.

5. *What the other kids think of him and how they treat him.* Sometimes teachers forget that a lot of fooling around in school is really a natural desire to "be one of the gang." Just getting some of these desires out in the open can do a lot toward directing students into a more profitable course of action.

This chapter has been a brief overview of an educational therapeutic approach to remedial reading. There are many more tests and diagnostic techniques that are available to the remedial teacher. For a fuller discussion of these, the reader is referred to Ashlock and Stephen's *Educational Therapy in the Elementary School.* For additional sources concerning buildup, the reader is referred to Edgington and Clements' *Indexed Bibliography on the Educational Management of Children with Learning Disabilities (Minimal Brain Dysfunction).*

CHAPTER 6

Instructional Approaches for Individuals
With Reading Difficulties

Historically, word recognition has been taught through three basic approaches:

1. The visual approach, sometimes known as the sight method
2. The auditory approach, sometimes known as the phonic method
3. A combination of approaches, sometimes known as the word analysis method

In this chapter, these traditional approaches are reviewed and approaches for remedial readers are proposed.

THE VISUAL APPROACH

The visual approach, or sight method, can be broken down into the ten broad categories described below.

Object Word Association

Both Comenius and Pestalozzi advocated this concrete method of building a basic sight vocabulary. The student is shown an object and the written form of its name. The pupil makes a simple association between the two.

Picture-Word Association

Comenius and Pestalozzi also made use of picture-word association in their teaching. Today, teaching materials of this type are available, as in the case of "Picture Word Cards" (Dolch, 1941), or the teacher can make picture word cards by pasting a picture on one side of an index card and writing the word on the reverse side of the card. Others who have stressed the importance of picture-word association are Mills (1964), Harris (1962), Adams, Gray, and Reese (1949), and Roswell and Natchez (1964).

Context Clues

The use of context clues is the process of using known words as a basis for making intelligent guesses at unknown words. For example, take the sentence, "The farmer painted the barn red." If the child knows all the words except *painted,* he might be able to guess this word correctly. Some authorities who have dealt with this aspect of word recognition are Betts (1957), Roswell and Natchez (1964), Kottmeyer (1959), and Patterson (1930).

Structural Clues

The child uses language structure clues when he figures out an unfamiliar word "just because it fits" into the sentence. For instance, in the sentence, "The boy ran up the hill" the word *ran* may be unfamiliar, but the child already knows *run.* Due to his knowledge of spoken English, he may make the correct substitution. Betts has called attention to "language-rhythm clues" (1957, p. 596).

Kinesthetic Method

Gray (1956), Fernald (1943), Scott and Thompson (1962), Money (1962), and Roswell and Natchez (1964) have made references to the use of the kinesthetic method of word recognition. The child may go through a variety of tactile-kinesthetic or kinesthetic activities such as tracing the word with his finger, tracing on a chalkboard, tracing with a stylus, tracing with a pencil, tracing in the air, etc.

Configuration

The child uses the shape of the word to help him remember it. This is a rudimentary perceptual skill and soon needs to be supplemented by more advanced word recognition methods. There are three general types of configuration skills.

GENERAL SHAPE. Among those calling attention to the child's use of the general shape of a word have been Mills (1964), Betts (1957), Scott and Thompson (1962), Gates (1947), Harris (1962), and Kottmeyer (1959). These authors usually referred to the "total shape," the "general characteristics," the "general configuration," or "the shape and length" of the word.

SPECIAL CHARACTERISTICS. Mills (1964, p. 4) discusses the child's "use of striking characteristics of words." Scott and Thompson (1962, p. 21) stated that children notice "unusual characteristics of the word—height of letters, parts of letters that fall below the line, or slant lines. . . ."

ESSENTIAL DISTINGUISHING FEATURES. Gates (1947, p. 244) noted that sometimes children are required to make use of "The absolutely essential distinguishing features of very similar words, as in the case of *house, horse; won, win; war, was.*"

Large Known Parts in Words

Russell (1949, p. 207) said, ". . . if children know *glass,* they make a good guess at *class.*"

Small Words in Larger Words

Bond and Bond (1943, p. 153) said that the knowledge of small words in larger words is a "useful and rapid technique for word recognition." Compound words such as *cowboy* and *fireman* might also be included in this classification.

Systematic Study of the Word

The child should be taught to examine words carefully in a left-to-right direction (Bond and Bond, 1943). This might help prevent reversals which may occur when the word is attacked as a whole.

Syllabication

The child breaks the words down into syllables, rather than other types of word parts (Bond and Bond, 1943).

THE AUDITORY APPROACH

Teaching by the sight method is an important way to *start* the child on his way to reading. But sight words alone will not take him far. To quote from "Learning to Read: A Report of a Conference of Reading Experts" (1963, p. 201).

> It is not true that our schools, in general, use primarily a "sight-word" method. It is not true that our schools, in general, do not teach phonics.
>
> We hold that reading cannot be taught through "sight-words" (look-say) alone. Such teaching would require our children to memorize, word by word, the mass of printed words. No reading authority advocates so impossible a procedure.
>
> We consider phonics one of the essential skills that help children identify printed words that they have not seen before and then understand the meaning that those words represent. Without phonics most children cannot become self-reliant, discriminating, efficient readers.

Visual perception, of central importance in the visual approach, is also important in the auditory approach. The child must correctly see the visual element before he learns to associate it with its sound.

Good auditory perception (or auditory discrimination) must be achieved before the child can really benefit from phonic instruction. The importance of auditory discrimination has been noted by Harris (1961, 1962, 1963), Betts (1957), Fernald (1943), Stern and Gould (1965), Dechant (1964), Heilman (1961), Wilson and Robeck (1965), Kirk (1940), Gray (1948), Robinson (1946), Grant and Karlin (1964), and Robinson (1957). Betts (1957) has treated thoroughly the development of auditory discrimination in the normal reading process. Harris (1961) and Ashlock and Stephen (1966) have drawn up guide lines for developing auditory discrimination in children who have learning problems.

Methods of phonic instruction are many and diverse, but most include the following areas.

Vowels

A *vowel* is one of the following letters: *a, e, i, o, u,* and *y* when *y* takes the place of the vowel *i*. Short vowel sounds are usually taught before long vowel sounds.

Consonants

A *consonant* is any letter that is not a vowel. Consonants which have only one sound are usually taught first. Consonants with more than one sound (such as *c* and *g*) are usually taught later.

Letter Combinations

Letter combinations consist of the following:
1. *Blends.* A blend is the fusing together of two or more letter sounds without any letter losing its individual sound. *Bl* is an example of a consonant blend. *Bi* is an example of a consonant-vowel blend.
2. *Digraphs.* A digraph consists of two letters which blend together to make one sound. *Ch* is an example of a consonant digraph. *Oa* is an example of a vowel digraph.
3. *Diphthongs.* A diphthong consists of two vowel letters blended together to make one compounded sound. Examples: *oi* and *oy*.

Rules For Sounding Out Words

The number of phonic rules varies radically from "method" to "method." The usual defect in most methods is that the rules are too many and too involved. The child who needs the rules most is seldom able to memorize them, and even less able to apply them. The child who can use the rules best is too often the child who has little need of them in the first place.

For the teacher who lacks background in phonics, Betts' *Foundations of Reading Instruction* is recommended. Scott and Thompson's *Phonics in Listening, in Speaking, in Reading, in Writing* is suggested for the teacher who is interested in ideas for the classroom teaching of phonics in a variety of settings. Russell, Murphy, and Durrell's *Developing Spelling Power* is an excellent approach to teaching phonics in the spelling program (where it should probably be taught in the first place.)

Gans' *Fact and Fiction About Phonics* is a book for the parent who has questions such as, Why don't the schools teach phonics? or for the school board member who usually understands even less about the whole situation.

THE COMBINATION APPROACH

Most educators today advocate some type of combination approach. One approach may favor the visual method, but still recognize the importance of phonics. The reverse may be true of those who lean toward the phonic method. Also, most approaches include some type of *structural analysis** and almost all stress the importance of dictionary skills. A few approaches include some use of tactile-kinesthetic or kinesthetic techniques.

A Suggested Combination Approach for Remedial Readers

The Ashlock Inventory of Word Attack Skills (Ashlock, (1968) and *The Teacher's Manual for the Ashlock Inventory of Word Attack Skills* (Ashlock, 1968) together form an experimental program to be used in the diagnostic teaching of word attack skills to remedial readers.

This program is built upon the following principles:
1. The combining of elements which are usually scattered throughout a developmental reading program. For instance, many related structural analysis skills are spread out through a reading program because the young child cannot deal with them all at one time. For the older remedial student, this need is not present.
2. The simplification of rules for sounding out words and the limiting of the number of such rules.
3. The simplification of syllabication rules and the limiting of the number of these rules.
4. The provision for informal (unstandardized) pre- and post-testing.

Structural analysis, as defined by Schubert (1964, p. 16), is "A method of analyzing a printed word to determine its pronunciation by identifying meaningful parts—roots, inflectional endings, syllables, prefixes and suffixes—which in turn may be blended into the sound of the word."

5. The foundation of the teaching program upon techniques which require inductive reasoning.

This program is predicated upon the following approaches:

1. Used as a pre-test, the *Ashlock Inventory of Word Attack Skills* is administered to the individual with reading difficulties.
2. If found to be necessary, the next step is the building of a rather extensive sight vocabulary. In this program, a basic sight vocabulary is built through the learning of object-word associations, picture-word associations, compound words, the use of context clues, and in extreme cases, the use of a tactile-kinesthetic approach.
3. Following this learning experience, the youngsters go into prescriptive teaching, using the tests in the AIWAS.
4. When the prescriptive teaching period is over, the teacher may again administer the AIWAS as a post-test if he feels that this information would be of instructional value.

The *Ashlock Inventory of Word Attack Skills* has been designed to test knowledge and use of word analysis skills in the following areas:

Adding *s, ed,* and *ing* to words.

Compound words

Rhyming

Adding *es, en, er,* and *est* to words.

Doubling the final consonant before adding *ed, ing, er,* and *est* to words.

Doubling the final consonant before adding *ed, ing, er,* and *est* to words.

Letter combinations: *ng, sh, ch, bl, cl, fl, gl, sl, br, cr, dr, fr, gr, pr, st, str, sw, sm, sp,* and *sn.*

The short *i* and long *e* sounds of *y.*

Nouns

Describing words

Changing a noun to a describing word by adding *y.*

Adding *ly* to a word to make it fit into the sentence structure.

Changing the *y* to *i* before adding *ed, es, er,* or *est.*

Long and short vowel sounds.

Final *e* rule.

Rule for sounding a single vowel at the beginning or in the middle of the word.

Rule for sounding a single vowel that comes at the end of a word.

Rule for sounding out a word that has two vowels together.

Rule for sounding out a word in which a single vowel is followed by *r*.

Rule for sounding out a word in which *a* is followed by *l* or *w*.

Letter combinations: *oo, ow, ou, oy,* and *oi.*

Root words

Common prefixes

Common suffixes

Syllabication (syllabification):

    Syllable perception

    Rule for dividing words into syllables when there are double consonants in the middle of a word.

    Rule for dividing words into syllables when the first vowel letter is followed by two different consonants.

    Rule for dividing words into syllables when the first vowel letter is followed by one consonant.

    Rule for dividing words into syllables when the *le* at the end of a word is preceded by a consonant.

Accent:

    Accent perception

    Rule for placing the accent in a word in which the last syllable is made up of a consonant followed by *y.*

    Rule for placing the accent in words which begin with the syllables *de, re, be, ex, in,* and *a.*

    Rule for placing the accent in words which end in the syllable *le* plus the preceding consonant.

    Rule for placing the accent in words which end with the syllables *es, er, ing, ed, est,* and *en.*

    Rule for placing the accent in words which end with the syllables *es, er, ing, ed, est,* and *en.*

    Rule for placing the accent in words made up of root words and suffixes.

Dictionary skills:

Location skills
Pronunciation skills
Meaning skills

VISUAL-AUDITORY APPROACHES

Initial Teaching Alphabet

The ITA, originally known as the *Augmented Roman Alphabet*, consists of forty-four instead of the usual twenty-six alphabetic symbols. In the ITA, each symbol represents only one sound. Once the child has mastered the forty-four symbols, it is simply a matter of blending them to form words.

Special alphabets have been in use for at least 400 years. Sir James Pitman began work on ITA in 1960, in London. The method is a total language arts approach. From the beginning, the child does handwriting, spelling, and engages in creative writing activities as well as reading.

The Downing Readers, published in England, was the first set of books printed in ITA. The books are attractive and well prepared. The *Early-to-Read* ITA Program is the ITA series prepared for use in this country. In content, the books are designed to appeal to the child's imagination rather than having him read about everyday experiences. Both of these series are available from Industrial Teaching Alphabet Publications.

Eventually, the child has to transfer from the *Initial Teaching Alphabet* to the regular alphabet. How easy this will be depends upon how flexible the child is.

This approach can be used with remedial readers. It may have the attraction of being "something different" in which the remedial student can have a "second chance." But the transfer to the traditional alphabet may present more problems to the remedial reader than to the average student.

Words In Color

This method, originally developed for the teaching of foreign phonic languages, has been adapted for the teaching of partially-phonic English. Where the ITA tries to solve the problem of the partially-phonic nature of English through the use of a special alphabet, *Words in Color* tries to accomplish the same goal through the use of different colors to represent different phonic elements.

Different colors represent the different sounds of English. By having the child associate one sound with one color, the teacher has taken some of the guesswork out of the child's learning task. By using color instead of a special alphabet, it is not necessary to change the spelling of words when transferring to regular print.

Some Thoughts About Visual-Auditory Approaches

These approaches seem to be based upon some fairly sound educational principles, but the transfer problem is worrisome.

Quick Success

At least theoretically, these approaches are structured so as to give the youngster a measure of success early in the reading experience.

Early Independence

The child is expected to achieve some measure of independence quickly. If such a method is to be successful with the remedial reader, this feeling of early independence in reading should be very important to him.

Decreased Importance of Memory

Both methods place a minimal emphasis upon the role of memory in the learning process. Once the youngster has learned the basic symbols or colors, most of the intellectual requirements are of a more insightful, more aggressive nature.

It's Different

The unusual nature of the methods give the remedial reader another chance at reading. The novelty of the methods sometimes appeals to the discouraged reader.

The Transfer

The student eventually has to transfer back to the traditionally written alphabet. How well the remedial youngster can do this, is a question still to be faced. Significant research findings are very much needed in this area.

TACTILE-KINESTHETIC APPROACHES

Tactile-kinesthetic approaches are generally based upon the theory that the use of touch and muscle movement reinforce learning which ordinarily takes place through the visual or visual-auditory avenues of learning. Tactile-kinesthetic activities can be many and varied, as outlined by Ashlock and Stephen (1966). The classic tactile-kinesthetic approach is that of Fernald (1943). Her method, only briefly outlined here, consisted of the following stages:

1. The word is written for the child. A crayon is used, and the letters are large. The child says the word as he traces it with his finger. The child does this until he can correctly write the word as a unit without looking at the copy. The youngster then writes the word in the story that he is composing. After the story is written, it is typed for him, and he reads it.
2. Eventually, the teacher writes the word for the child, he looks at the word, says it to himself, and then writes the word from memory. The word is then used in context.
3. The youngster looks at the printed word, says it to himself, and writes it from memory. The word does not have to be written out for him. Fernald (1943, p. 51) found that it was at this stage that the youngster began to want to read books.
4. The child becomes able to figure out new words because of their similarity to words (or parts of words) that have already been learned. This is the stage that makes some reading specialists a little uneasy. What if this "transfer" does not take place?

The tactile-kinesthetic approach to learning has too many

facets to be adequately covered in a book of this scope. It is recommended that all remedial teachers read Fernald's book, *Remedial Techniques in Basic School Subjects*.

An interesting modification of the tracing technique has been developed at the Reading Laboratory at Illinois State University. A tracing frame is made from masonite and covered with screen wire. Paper is laid over this wire, and the word is written with a crayon. The effect is one of an embossed copy, the roughness of the copy further stimulating the sense of touch.

Some Thoughts About Tactile-Kinesthetic Approaches

Last Resort

Some form of tactile-kinesthetic approach is usually the last resort for the remedial reader. It seems that multisensory stimulation gets some results with certain problem readers.

It's Different

The novelty of the approach appeals to some youngsters.

Novelty Short-Lived

The novelty often expires early in the process. Sometimes the drudgery of the tactile-kinesthetic process exasperates both student and teacher.

Vocabulary Not Limited

Because of the stories that the youngster writes for his reading material, he can use any words that he can speak. This keeps the older reader from having to work with a "baby" vocabulary.

Interest is There

The youngster writes stories about anything in which he is interested, so there is a certain amount of built-in motivation in the method.

EXPERIENCE APPROACHES

For the remedial reader, often discouraged after repeated

failures with books, it is sometimes better to have the young-ster read about experiences in which he has had a part. And, since some remedial readers are of low-average intelligence, this concreteness of approach is sometimes called for.

In experience approaches, the child usually dictates read-ing material concerning his experiences or writes such material with the help of the teacher or another child. It should be kept in mind that the experiences can be either concrete or vicarious. In some cases, the teacher selects already written material which is closely related to the experiences of the child.

Student interests upon which the reading teacher might capitalize are

Trips taken
Movies seen
Television programs seen
Books read
Daydreams
Hobbies
Sports
Movie stars
Public figures
History
Science experiments performed
Pictures drawn
Creative writing experiences
Creative dramatic experiences
Using recipes
Keeping diaries
Keeping records
Labeling collections
Reading maps
Interviews done

Some Thoughts About Experience Approaches

Motivating

The motivational value of the experience approach is very

real. This approach has been the *beginning* of many a successful remedial reading program.

Not a Steady Diet

The experience approach can seldom be used as a steady reading diet for a child. This is so because it is a rare teacher who can "incidentally" teach a youngster all his reading skills through an experience approach. Do not keep up the experience approach after the child has lost interest in it. This can result in a situation similar to the joke about two little boys on a field trip. One said, "Look at that!" "Don't 'rook," answered the other, "If you 'rook, you have to 'rite, and if you 'rite, you have to read." At its best, the experience approach is used between sessions of reading from books. The variety helps keep the reading lessons alive.

The Importance of Books

When using the experience method, it is good to keep in mind how important a book is to a child. No matter how many experience stories a child can learn to read, he often still considers himself to be a failure until he can read a book.

MOTIVATIONAL APPROACHES

Almost any method of teaching a child to read can be a motivational approach, depending upon the interests of the youngster. The importance of the motivational appeal of a method should never be overlooked when working with a discouraged student. Included in this section are descriptions of two examples of motivational approaches to reading instruction.

Programmed Learning

Most programmed learning is based upon three general principles: (1) The student is engaged in active, as opposed to passive, learning; (2) The student is kept informed about the accuracy of his responses; (3) The student works at his own rate.

Examples of Programmed Reading Materials

The Basal Progressive Choice Reading Program (Woolman, 1962): Programmed reading readiness material.

Teachall Reading Course (Publishers Company, 1962): A programmed set of cards to be used in the Teachall teaching machine for the learning of 48 nouns.

First Steps in Reading (Teaching Machine Inc., 1962): A programmed primer that can be used in a machine by beginning readers under a parent's direction.

Dialogue I (Brogan and Hotchkiss, 1963): A programmed book and tape recordings to be used in teaching phonics.

Lessons for Self-Instruction in Basic Skills (Bostwick and Midloch, 1963): Booklets on "Reading Interpretations" and on "Reference Skills" for use at the junior high school level.

How to Improve Your Reading and Vocabulary Growth (Abraham, 1963): A programmed booklet for the junior high level.

Programmed Reading Books (Buchanan *et al.*, 1963-1964): A set of programmed reading books which has a strong motivational appeal.

Michigan Successive Discrimination Reading Program (Smith, 1965): A general language arts program based upon the programmed instruction principles. This program is for the teaching of English speaking children and adults.

Individualized Reading*

Individualized reading is a term which refers to any type of reading instruction in which each child works on reading material at his own level, progressing at his own rate, and in which he receives a certain amount of individual attention from the teacher. Children's self-selection of materials is often a part of individualized reading, but is not necessarily basic to the individualized approach.

There are any number of different types of individualized

*From an address delivered by the author at the December 2, 1964, meeting of the Franklin Park Chapter of the Illinois Classroom Teachers' Association in Franklin Park, Illinois.

reading. In this section, some of the more common character-istics of an individualized reading program are summarized.

A wide variety of reading materials must be provided. The number of different titles will vary according to the grade level. More titles at more levels will have to be provided as the children move into the upper grades due to the progressive widening span of reading levels. Materials should not be limited to textbooks. The individualized reading collection should include trade books, newspapers, magazines, teacher-made materials, and reading materials which the children themselves have written.

A reading period of sufficient length must be provided. At least an hour and a half a day should be devoted to the teaching of reading. Some of this time may be devoted to material from subject areas. For instance, after the child has done a certain amount of silent reading, he may turn to seat work which is related to arithmetic, language arts, social studies, health, art, etc.

Independent work habits must become highly developed. The teacher, during the reading period, will be working with only one child at a time. During this time the other children must be *meaningfully* occupied. This requires a daily planning period during which the teacher and the children decide how each child is to be independently occupied during much of the reading period. At this time, the teacher may also give the children any special directions which may be required for their independent work.

Good discipline must be maintained. No matter how interested the children may be in the independent work provided, there are going to be some rough spots. The teacher will need to have the type of discipline which can be maintained without constantly interrupting the one child who is reading to the teacher.

A successful individualized reading program depends upon good record keeping. Records are of two types: a list of the books read by the child during the year, and an anecdotal record of the child's progress and interests during each oral reading session with the teacher. The teacher should note how well the child is reading, how well he is comprehending what he reads, how his interests are *developing*, and what his needs are in the different areas of word analysis.

The teaching of word-analysis skills must not be neglected. The teacher must be careful that the teaching of word analysis skills is not slighted. These skills can be taught to each child as they are needed, or to small groups of children who are in need of such instruction. The small group approach seems to be more economical.

Evaluation is important. In the individual situation, evaluation can be done more personally and more frequently than in a large group. Children need answers to such questions as, Am I picking books that are right for me? Am I doing all right? What do I need to learn next?

Parent understanding is essential. Before individualized reading is initiated, the parents need to have every opportunity to understand the program. Parents tend to become upset when children do not use basal textbooks. The purpose and methods of individualized reading instruction need to be explained (more than once) to the parents involved.

Reading can be individualized in five ways. These can be used individually, or in various combinations.

1. Reading Level

Each child is guided into using reading material at his own level. He may have a fairly free choice of reading materials as long as they are neither too difficult nor too easy for his present level of development. Commercial materials such as the following lend themselves to individualized reading instruction at a variety of reading levels.

S.R.A. Reading Laboratories (Parker, 1957-1964): These sets come in different grade-level ranges from primary through the adult levels. The child can read for comprehension, the development of word analysis skills, and the development of reading rate at his own level. The motivational value is high.

Gates-Peardon Reading Exercises (Gates and Peardon, 1963): These are individual booklets which are used in developing reading comprehension. There are different sets of books for work on (1) general reading ability, (2) what the story is about, (3) remembering details, and (4) reading to follow directions. Grade levels range from one through seven. The interest level is high, and the use of the books is usually effective.

New Practice Readers (Stone *et al.*, 1962): These reading books provide an introductory vocabulary exercise, a reading selection, and a recall comprehension exercise for each selection. Grade levels range from second through eighth. Motivation level is very high.

Reader's Digest Skill Builders (Reader's Digest Services, 1958-1966): Grade levels are from first through eighth. The material is interesting, but of limited depth.

Standard Test Lessons in Reading (McCall and Crabbs, 1961): These books are used for the improvement of reading comprehension and reading rate. Grade levels are third to seventh.

Controlled Reader (Educational Developmental Laboratories, 1959-1967): This is a machine used to flash a story on the screen at an even, controlled speed. Grade levels range from readiness into the adult level. Motivation is usually very high— especially for boys.

2. Reading Rate

Often, children reading on the same grade level may vary significantly according to their reading rates. Research has shown that a good reading rate and a good level of comprehension often go together. Therefore, we may wish to individualize the reading instruction so that a child learns to read at the best rate for him, and for the type of material that he is reading. It may be wished to teach a child to skim and/or scan as well as to read. Of the commercially available materials, the author has found the *Controlled Reader*, and the rate builders in the *SRA Reading Laboratory*, and the *Standard Test Lessons in Reading* to be useful for this purpose.

3. Individual Attention

It is often found that the extra attention received in an individualized reading program is important to a childs reading development. Even though the child may read orally to the teacher only every three or four days, some educators feel that this attention is much to be desired.

4. Emotional Needs

If a child is allowed to make some of his own reading selections, much can be learned about his emotional needs. Through his reading selections, a child might show some of his needs for a more secure family life, for having more friends, for expressing a need for independence, and any number of other needs.

5. Interests

When a child is allowed some choice of his own reading materials, he can concentrate on pursuing special interests. Some educators believe that this may result in a narrow development of reading interests, but the author does not think that there is any great danger of this. Usually, once a child has fully pursued an interest in a topic, he will move on to wider horizons.

Some Thoughts About Motivational Approaches

Motivation is Important

Trying to motivate the poor reader is the least we can do before we drag him through remedial instruction. As adults, we sometimes forget the importance of motivation until we undertake something like going on a diet or giving up smoking.

Not Always Possible

It is not always possible to motivate a youngster. If this is the case, the teacher has two choices: force the child, or give up.

CHAPTER 7

Instructional Materials for Individuals With Reading Difficulties

$\mathbf{M}$ATERIALS FOR REMEDIAL readers can be divided into three general classes as follows:

1. Buildup materials
2. Skill building materials
3. Remedial reading materials

Buildup materials are those used to improve a youngster's basic learning processes. Buildup materials may be used to improve a youngster's auditory perception, eye-hand coordination, visual perception, etc.

Skill building materials are those used to give the reader the basic skills that he needs in order to become an independent reader. This type of material is used to develop such skills as a basic sight vocabulary, word attack skills, comprehension skills, oral reading skills, and improved reading rate.

Remedial reading materials are those in which the child uses his basic learning processes and reading skills to get information and enjoyment out of reading. For the average student, this is usually a pleasure and a looked-forward-to experience. For the remedial reader, it is too often a dreaded and distasteful task. For reading material to be successfully used with remedial readers it should usually have a well controlled vocabulary, but an interest level which is higher than that on which the youngster is able to read. These are what are usually called "high interest—low vocabulary" books.

BUILDUP MATERIALS

Most of the materials listed here were originally designed for children in the primary and intermediate grades. Whenever material seems to be especially suited for more mature individuals, the name of the material is followed by an *M*. If no grade level is designated, the material is adaptable for a wide range of instructional levels.

Auditory Perception

The following is a list of materials which may be used to improve a youngster's auditory perception:

Rhyming-workbook activities, Levels 1 and 2—*Primary* (Continental Press)

Sound Boxes (Daigger)

Listening Time, Creative Music for Exceptional Children, Classroom Rhythms, Listening Skills for Pre-Readers, Vols. 1-4; Songs for Children with Special Needs, Vols. 1-3; Listening with Mr. Bunny Big Ears—*Primary* (Educational Records)

Come and Hear—*Primary* (Follett)

Objects That Rhyme (Hammett)

Listen and Do—*Primary* (Houghton Mifflin)

Objects That Rhyme, Rhyming Pictures, Rhyming Puzzles—*Primary* (Ideal)

Rhythm band instruments—*Primary* (Paine)

A Reading Readiness Program for the Mentally Retarded—*Primary Level* (Parkinson)

Lift-off to Reading—*Grades 1-6* (Science Research)

Sounds Around Us, Poetry Time (record albums)—*Primary* (Scott, Foresman)

Rhyming-Sound Cards (Steck)

Peabody Language Development Kits—*Preschool, Grade 4* (American Guidance)

Sound Effects—*M* (Audio Fidelity)

Listening Aids Through the Grades—*Primary, Intermediate* (Teachers College Press)

Rhythm band instruments—*Primary* (Beckley-Cardy, Creative Playthings, School Playthings)

Sound Cylinders (Creative Playthings)

Reading Exercises; Level O—*Primary* (Committee on Diagnostic Reading Tests)

What's Its Name?—*Kindergarten, Intermediate* (University of Illinois Press)

Eye-Hand Coordination

The following is a list of materials which may be used to improve a youngster's eye-hand coordination:

Climbing Equipment (Community)

Dressing Frames, Cylinder Blocks, Broad Stair, Pink Tower, Long Stair, Locks and Catch Boards, Cabinet of Geometric Insets, Metal Insets, Sandpaper Alphabet, Kindergarten Blocks (Daigger)

People and Animal Puzzles, Shapes Puzzles, Stencils Color Cued Control Paper, Colored Inch Cubes, Colored Inch Cube Designs, Designs in Perspective, Large Parquetry, Small Parquetry, Plain Inch Cubes (Developmental Learning Materials)

The Slingerland Kit—*Preschool, Intermediate* (Educators)

Magna-Sized Jigsaw Family Orthoball—*Primary* (Educational Research Associates)

Parquetry Design Blocks, Alphabet Inlay Puzzles, Colored Cubes, Large Beads and Laces, King Hardwood Inset Puzzle (Hammett)

Puzzle Inlays, Judyettes, Storyettes, Parquetry Blocks (Judy)

Motor-Ocular Training Packet (O'Connor)

Trace and Color, Stick 'em Pushouts—*Primary* (Platt & Munk)

Coordination Board (Sifo)

The Spatial Organization Series—*Primary* (Allied)

Montessori Granded Cylinder Set with Knobs, Montessori Geometric Problem Boards, Ben-G Reading Readiness Puzzles, Rubber Peg Board with 100 Holes, 100 Heavy-duty Beaded Pegs, Interlocking Train Blocks, Montessori Dressing Frame (Creative Playthings)

Reading Exercises: Level O—*Primary* (Committee on Diagnostic Reading Tests)

Visual Motor Skills-Workbook activities, Levels 1 and 2 (Continental Press)

Lacing Boot, Make-It Set, Jumbo Beads and Laces, Playschool Puzzles, Kinesthetic Alphabet (Stone)

Fruit and Animal Puzzles, Small Form Puzzles, Large Form Puzzles, Geometric Shapes in Color, Association Cards, "See and Say" Puzzle Cards, Configuration Cards, Ordinal Placement Board, Flip and Build, Concept Clocks in Color, "Show You Know—Then Go" Phonics Game, Fairbanks-Robinson Program—*Primary; Erie Program* (Teaching Resources)

Visual Perception

The following is a list of materials which may be used to improve a youngster's visual perception:

Filmstrips: Visual Perception Skills—*Primary* (Educational Records)

Frostig Program for the Development of Visual Perception (Follett)

Folding Perception Cards (Hammett)

Exercises to develop visual discrimination for letter and word forms (from) Getting Ready to Read—*Primary* (Houghton Mifflin)

Letter Cards, Large Letter Cards, Basic Letter Shapes (Ideal)

A Reading Readiness Program for the Mentally Retarded Primary Level (Parkinson)

Lift-Off to Reading—*Grades 1-6* (Science Research)

Peabody Language Development Kits—*Preschool, Grade 4* (American Guidance)

The Spatial Organization Series—*Primary* (Allied)

Reading Exercises: Level O—*Primary* (Committee on Diagnostic Reading Tests)

Visual Discrimination Independent Activities-Workbook activities, Levels, 1 and 2; Seeing Likenesses and Differences, Levels 1-3 (Continental Press)

Color Tablets, Sorting Box Combination, Geometric Form Cards (Daigger)

Filmstrips for Readiness (Educational Development Laboratories)

SKILL BUILDING MATERIALS

Due to the fact that the "grade levels" differ from publisher to publisher because of the use of different readability formulas, the grade levels given here should be considered only approximate.

Basic Sight Vocabulary

The following is a list of materials which can be used to develop a basic sight vocabulary:

A Reading Vocabulary for the Primary Grades (Teachers College Press)

A Core Vocabulary Consisting of a Basic Vocabulary for Grades 1-8 and Advanced Vocabulary for Grades 9-13 (Educational Developmental Laboratories)

Beginning to Read Picture Dictionary—*Primary* (Follett)

Picture Word Cards, Popper Words, Basic Sight Cards, Group Word Teaching Game, Sight Phrase Cards (Garrard)

Picture Words for Beginners (Hammett) Magna-Sized Flash Cards (Mafex)

Flash Words-Sets 1-2, Picture Words for Beginners, Picture Word Builder, Words That Go Together—*Primary* (Milton Bradley)

Sight Phrase Cards (School Playthings) Basic Word Cards, Phrase-O Game, Basic Phrase Flash Cards, Practice Book in Phrase Reading (Steck)

Word Attack Skills

The following is a list of materials which can be used to develop word attack skills (*M* = mature):

Independent Word Perception—*Primary, M* (Association Instructional Materials)

School Edition of the Sound Way to Easy Reading—*Primary* (Bremner-Davis)

Word Attack Series—*Grades 2-4* (Teachers College Press)

Beginning Sounds—Workbook activities, Levels 1 and 2—*Primary* (Continental Press)

Remedial Training for Children with Specific Disability in Reading, Spelling, and Penmanship—*Primary, Intermediate* (Educators)

Phonetic Keys to Reading—with accompanying workbooks—*Primary, Intermediate* (Economy)

Bulletin Board of Basic Phonics, Third Syllable Game, Primary Picture Alphabet, The Magic Vowel, Match the Vowel (Educational Aids)

What the Letters Say, Consonant Lotto, Vowel Lotto, Take the Syllable Game, Group Sounding Game (Garrard)

The Magic of Sounds (Hamilton)

Consonant Pictures for Pegboard, Initial and Final Consonant Charts, Blend and Digraphs for Pegboard, Blends and Digraph Charts, Vowel Charts, Vowel Pictures for Pegboard, Phonic Drill Cards, Phonic Talking Letters, Phonic Word Builder—*Primary* (Ideal)

Reading with Phonics—*Primary* (Lippincott)

Phonics We Use—*Grades 1-6* (Lyons and Carnahan)

Phonics Skill Texts—*Grades 1-5* (Merrill, Charles E.)

Phonetic Word Builder, Embecco Phonetic Drill Cards, Phonetic Word Wheel, Phonetic Quizmo (Milton Bradley)

Corrective Reading Study Drill Cards, *M*, Corrective Reading Roll-up Charts, *M* (O'Connor)

Word Blends, Word Prefixes, Word Suffixes, Phonic Rummy, Phonetic Quizmo, Phonetic Word Drill Cards, Picture-Phonic Cards, Phonic Fun Workbooks (Paine)

The Phonovisual Method—*Primary - 4* (Phonovisual)

Attack-o-Word Kit, Initial Consonant Sounds, Vowel Sounds, Phonetic Word Drill Set (School Playthings)

Filmstrips for Practice in Phonetic Skills—*Primary, Intermediate* (Scott, Foresman)

Reading Essentials Teaching Aids, Let's Listen Cards, Phono-Word Wheels (Steck)

Word Attack Skills—*Primary* (Wahr)

Eye and Ear Fun—*Primary, Intermediate* (Webster Division of McGraw-Hill)

Word Attack, Comprehension, Oral Reading, and Reading Rate Skills

The following is a list of materials which can be used to develop word attack, comprehension, oral reading and reading rate skills:

Mott Basic Language Skills Program—*Grades 1-9, M* (Allied)

Know Your World, *M* (American Education)

Using the Context, Working with Sounds, Following Directions, Locating the Answers, Getting the Facts—*Grades 1-6* (Barnell Loft)

The Sullivan Reading Program—*Grades 1-8, M* (Behavioral Research)

Reading Aids Through the Grades—*Primary, Intermediate;* Test Lessons in Primary Reading (Teachers College Press)

Teen Agers Prepare for Work, *M* (Carson)

And Hereby Hangs the Tale, *M* (CENCO)

Reading Exercises: Levels 0-III—*Grade 1 Adult, M.* (Committee on Diagnostic Reading Tests)

Controlled Reader—*Grades 1-14, M;* Comprehension Power Paragraphs and Sentences—*Grades 3-6, M* (Educational Developmental Laboratories)

World History Study Lessons for High School Slow Learners, *M;* American History Study Lessons in Our Nation's History for Elementary and Junior High School Slow Learners, *M;* Success in Language for Elementary and Junior High School Slow Learners, *M;* Success in Language for High School Slow Learners, *M;* The Turner-Livingston Reading Series, *M* (Follett)

Vanguard *M,* Perspectives, *M;* Accent: U.S.A., *M; Basic Reading* Skills for Junior High School Use, *M;* Basic Reading Skills for High School Use, *M;* Adventures with Animals, *M;* Around the World in Eighty Days, *M* (Scott, Foresman)

Tachist-0-Film Kits, *M* (Learning Through Seeing) Reading for Meaning—*Grades 4-11, M* (Lippincott)

The Targer Series, *M;* Pete Saves the Day, *M;* I Live in Many Places, *M;* The Old Shoe Mystery, *M* (Mafex)

Classroom Reading Clinic (Webster Division of McGraw-Hill)

Developing Potential Reading Ability—*Grades 4-12* (McQueen)

Reading Skill Texts—*Grades 1-12;* Diagnostic Reading Workbooks—*Grades, 1-6* (Merrill, Charles E.)

News for You, *M* (New Readers Press)

Springboards, *M* (Portal)

Getting Ready for Pay Day, *M;* I Want a Job, *M;* On the Job, *M;* Finding Ourselves', *M;* Happy Housekeepers, *M;* The Getting Along Series, *M;* Our Reader, *M;* (Frank E. Richards)

Reading in High Gear, *M;* New Rochester Occupational Reading Series, *M;* (Science Research)

The Read and Succeed Series, *M* (Silver Burdett)

Functional Basic Reading—*Grades 1-5, M* (Stanwix)

My Country, *M;* Learning and Writing English, *M;* I Want to Read and Write, *M;* Veteran's Reader, *M;* How to Read Better, *M* (Steck)

Conquests in Reading—*Intermediate* (Webster Division of McGraw-Hill)

REMEDIAL READING MATERIALS

The following lists of books have been found to be of interest to individuals who have reading difficulties. The interest and grade levels should be considered to be approximations.

Grade 1

READING LEVEL	INTEREST LEVEL	AUTHOR	TITLE	PUBLISHER
1	1-6	Battle	*Jerry*	Benefic
1	1-6	Battle	*Jerry Goes Fishing*	Benefic
1	1-6	Battle	*Jerry Goes Riding*	Benefic
1	2-3	Beim	*Thin Ice*	Morrow
1-2	1-5	Berenstain	*The Big Honey Hunt*	Random
1	1-3	Branley	*Big Tracks, Little Tracks*	Crowell
1-2	1-4	Branley	*The Moon Seems to Change*	Crowell
1	1-3	Bright	*Where is Willy?*	Golden
1	2-3	Brown	*Red Light, Green Light*	Doubleday
1	2-3	Brown	*Wheel on the Chimney*	Lippincott
1	1-6	Cerf	*Bennett Cerf's Book of Laughs*	Random
1-2	1-7	Cerf	*Book of Riddles*	Random
1-2	1-7	Cerf	*More Riddles*	Random
1	1-3	Chandler	*Cowboy Andy*	Random
1	1-9	Chandler	*Cowboy Sam*	Benefic
1	1-3	Chandler	*Cowboy Sam and Big Bill*	Benefic
1	1-4	Chandler	*Cowboy Sam and Dandy*	Benefic
1	1-9	Chandler	*Cowboy Sam and Freddy*	Benefic
1	1-4	Chandler	*Cowboy Sam and Flop*	Benefic
1	1-3	Chandler	*Cowboy Sam and Miss Lily*	Benefic
1	1-9	Chandler	*Cowboy Sam and Porky*	Benefic
1	1-9	Chandler	*Cowboy Sam and Shorty*	Benefic
1	1-6	Cordts	*Tommy O'Toole and Larry*	Benefic
1	1-4	Davis	*Pinkie*	Garrard
1	1-4	Dolch	*Friendly Birds*	Steck
1	1-5	Dolch	*Once There was a Monkey*	McGraw

1	1-5	Dudley	*Hank and the Kitten*	Morrow
1	2-3	Eastman	*Are You My Mother?*	Random
1	1-3	Eastman	*Go, Dog, Go!*	Random
1	1-8	Eastman	*Sam and the Firefly*	Random
1-2	1-5	Elkin	*The King's Wish*	Random
1-2	1-5	Farley	*Little Black, a Pony*	Random
1	2-3	Flack	*Angus and the Cat*	Doubleday
1	2-3	Flack	*Angus and the Ducks*	Doubleday
1	2-3	Flack	*Angus Lost*	Doubleday
1	2-3	Flack	*Wait for William*	Houghton
1	2-3	Flack	*William and His Kitten*	Houghton
1	K-3	Fox	*Come to the Circus*	Reilly
1-2	1-4	Fox	*A Fox in the House*	Reilly
1-2	1-5	Freeman	*You Will Go to the Moon*	Random
1	1-5	Gates	*The Open Window*	Macmillan
1	1-6	Gates	*Three Little Elephants*	Macmillan
1	1-5	Gates	*Toby*	Macmillan
1	1-5	Gates	*Two Boys and a Tree*	Macmillan
1	1-4	Georgiady	*Gertie the Duck*	Follett
1-2	1-3	Greene	*I Want to Be an Animal Doctor*	Childrens
1-2	1-3	Greene	*I Want to Be a Carpenter*	Childrens
1-2	1-3	Greene	*I Want to Be a Fireman*	Childrens
1-2	1-3	Greene	*I Want to Be a Nurse*	Childrens
1-2	1-4	Greene	*I Want to Be a Policeman*	Childrens
1	2-3	Guilfoile	*Nobody Listens to Andrew*	Follett
1-2	1-5	Gurney	*The King, the Mice, and the Cheese*	Random
1-2	1-4	Heilbroner	*This is the House Where Jack Lives*	Harper
1	1-4	Heilbroner	*Robert, the Rose Horse*	Random
1	1-4	Hoff	*Albert the Albatross*	Harper
1	1-4	Hoff	*Chester*	Harper
1-2	1-4	Hoff	*Julius*	Harper
1	1-4	Hoff	*Oliver*	Harper
1	1-4	Hoff	*Stanley*	Harper
1	2-3	Huber	*The Ranch Book*	Macmillan
1	2-3	Huber	*Skags, the Milk Horse*	American
1	1-4	Huber	*I Know a Story*	Harper
1	1-3	Hurd	*Hurry, Hurry*	Harper
1	1-4	Hurd	*Last One Home Is a Green Pig*	Harper
1	2-9	Hurley	*Dan Frontier*	Benefic
1	2-9	Hurley	*Dan Frontier Goes Hunting*	Benefic
1	1-4	Hurley	*Dan Frontier with the Indians*	Benefic
1-2	1-4	Jordan	*Seeds by Wind and Water*	Crowell
1	1-3	Kessler	*Here Comes the Strikeout*	Harper
1	1-4	Krauss	*The Carrot Seed*	Harper
1-2	1-4	Kumin	*Eggs of Things*	Putnam
1	1-4	LaRue	*Tiny Toosey's Birthday*	Houghton
1	2-3	Lenski	*Cowboy Small*	Walck
1	2-3	Lenski	*The Little Airplane*	Walck
1	1-4	Lenski	*The Little Auto*	Walck
1	2-3	Lenski	*Papa Small*	Walck
1	2-9	Lent	*Straight Up*	Macmillan
1	1-3	LeSieg	*Ten Apples Up on Top*	Random

1-2	1-4	Lexau	*I Should Have Stayed in Bed*	Harper
1	1-3	Lexau	*That's Good, That's Bad*	Dial
1	1-4	Lexau	*Olaf is Late*	Dial
1	1-3	Lopshire	*Put Me in the Zoo*	Random
1-2	1-4	Lopshire	*How to Make Flibbers, Etc.*	Random
1	1-3	Martini	*What a Frog Can Do*	Reilly
1	2-3	McAuley	*Willie Duck*	Macmillan
1	1-5	McCall	*Bucky Button*	Benefic
1	1-5	McCall	*The Buttons and the Pet Parade*	Benefic
1	1-5	McCall	*The Buttons at the Farm*	Benefic
1	2-3	McCall	*The Buttons at the Zoo*	Benefic
1	1-2	McCall	*The Buttons See Things That Go*	Benefic
1-2	1-4	McClintock	*A Fly Went By*	Random
1	1-5	McClintock	*Stop That Ball*	Random
1-2	K-3	Minarik	*Father Bear Comes Home*	Harper
1	K-4	Minarik	*Little Bear's Friend*	Harper
1-2	K-3	Minarik	*Little Bear*	Harper
1-2	K-3	Minarik	*Little Bear's Visit*	Harper
1-2	K-4	Miner	*True Book of Plants We Know*	Childrens
1-2	1-4	Moore	*Little Racoon and the Outside World*	McGraw
1-2	1-4	Moore	*Little Racoon and the Thing in the Pool*	McGraw
1	1-4	Parker and O'Donnell	*Fall is Here*	Harper
1	1-4	Parker and O'Donnell	*Spring is Here*	Harper
1	1-4	Parker and O'Donnell	*Summer is Here*	Harper
1	1-4	Parker and O'Donnell	*Winter is Here*	Harper
1	1-4	Pearson	*Buttons and His Sunday Coat*	Steck
1	1-5	Phleger	*Ann Can Fly*	Random
1-2	1-5	Phleger	*Whales Go By*	Random
1-2	1-4	Platt	*Big Max*	Harper
1-2	K-4	Podendorf	*True Book of Animal Babies*	Childrens
1	2-3	Pratt and Meighen	*Story Time*	Singer
1	2-3	Pratt and Meighen	*Story Wagon*	Singer
1	1-3	Rey	*Curious George Flies a Kite*	Houghton
1-2	1-4	Seuss	*The Cat in the Hat*	Random
1	1-4	Seuss	*The Cat in the Hat Comes Back*	Random
1	1-4	Seuss	*One Fish, Two Fish, Red Fish, Blue Fish*	Random
1	1-4	Sharp	*Daffy*	Steck
1	1-3	Sharp and Young	*Downy Duck Grows Up*	Steck
1	1-3	Sharp and Young	*Watch Me*	Steck
1	1-3	Sharp and Young	*Who Are You?*	Steck
1	1-3	Sharp and Young	*Where is Cubby Bear?*	Steck

1	K-4	Stewart	*Funny Squirrel*	Reilly
1	1-3	Tensen	*Come to the Pet Shop*	Reilly
1-2	1-4	Thayer	*The Second-Story Giraffe*	Morrow
1	1-5	Thompson	*The House that Liked Sandwiches*	Putnam
1	2-3	Unwin	*Doughnuts for Lin*	Aladdin
1	K-4	Wiseman	*Morris Is a Cowboy*	Harper
1	1-5	Yoakam, *et al.*	*Making Storybook Friends*	Laidlaw
1	1-4	Yoakam, *et al.*	*On the Way to Storyland*	Laidlaw

Grade 2

READING LEVEL	INTEREST LEVEL	AUTHOR	TITLE	PUBLISHER
2-3	2-5	Adamson	*Old Man Up a Tree*	Abelard
2	3-4	Adelson	*All Ready for Winter*	McKay
2-3	1-5	Allen	*Everyday Animals*	Houghton
2-3	1-8	Allen	*Everyday Insects*	Houghton
2-3	1-6	Anderson	*Blaze and the Forest Fire*	Macmillan
2	1-4	Anderson	*Blaze and the Gypsies*	Macmillan
2	2-7	Anderson	*Squanto and the Pilgrims*	Harper
2	2-5	Barr	*Little Circus Dog*	Whitman, Albert
2	2-6	Battle	*Jerry Goes on a Picnic*	Benefic
2	3-4	Becker	*900 Buckets of Paint*	Abingdon
2	1-4	Beim	*Country Fireman*	Morrow
2	1-4	Beim	*Country Mailman*	Morrow
2	2-6	Beim	*Country Train*	Morrow
2	1-4	Beim	*The Little Igloo*	Harcourt
2	2-7	Beim	*Tim and the Tool Chest*	Morrow
2	1-4	Beim	*Two Is a Team*	Harcourt
2	1-4	Bell	*Andy and Mr. Wagner*	Abingdon
2	2-6	Berres	*The Sea Hunt*	Harr
2	2-5	Berres	*Treasure Under the Sea*	Harr
2-3	2-6	Blough	*Who Lives in This House?*	McGraw
2-3	2-6	Blough	*Who Lives in This Meadow?*	McGraw
2	1-4	Bonsall	*The Case of the Hungry Stranger*	Harper
2	1-4	Bonsall	*The Case of the Cat's Meow*	Harper
2	1-4	Branley	*Mickey's Magnet*	Crowell
2	1-4	Branley	*The Sun: Our Nearest Star*	Crowell
2	3-4	Bright	*Georgie*	Doubleday
2	3-4	Bromhall	*Mary Ann's First Picture*	Knopf
2	3-4	Brown	*Little Lost Lamb*	Doubleday
2-3	1-5	Brown	*Sparkie and Puff Ball*	Scribner
2	3-4	Buff	*Dash and Dart*	Viking
2	3-4	Buff	*Elf Owl*	Viking
2	3-4	Buff	*Hurry, Skurry and Flurry*	Viking
2-3	2-5	Bulla	*A Ranch for Danny*	Crowell
2	2-8	Burton	*The Little House*	Houghton
2-3	2-5	Carter	*True Book of Oceans*	Childrens
2	3-4	Caudill	*Up and Down the River*	Holt
2	3-9	Chandler	*Cowboy Sam and the Fair*	Benefic
2	3-9	Chandler	*Cowboy Sam and Freddy*	Benefic

2	3-9	Chandler	*Cowboy Sam and the Rodeo*	Benefic
2	3-9	Chandler	*Cowboy Sam and the Rustlers*	Benefic
2	1-4	Chandler	*Cowboy Sam and Sally*	Benefic
2	3-6	Clark	*Poppy Seed Cakes*	Doubleday
2	3-4	Creekmore	*Little Fu*	Macmillan
2	3-4	Creekmore	*Lokoshi*	Macmillan
2	3-4	Danneker	*Happy, Hero and Judge*	Abingdon
2	1-6	D'Aulaire	*Don't Count Your Chicks*	Doubleday
2	3-4	Davis	*Timothy Turtle*	Hale
2	3-4	Delafield	*Mrs. Mallard's Ducklings*	Hale
2	3-9	Disney	*Donald Duck and His Nephews*	Heath
2	2-7	Dolch	*Animal Stories*	Garrard
2	2-6	Dolch	*Circus Stories*	Garrard
2	3-9	Dolch	*Dog Stories*	Garrard
2	2-6	Dolch	*Elephant Stories*	Garrard
2	2-4	Dolch	*Folk Stories*	Garrard
2	2-7	Dolch	*More Dog Stories*	McGraw
2	2-6	Dolch	*Pueblo Stories*	Garrard
2	2-6	Dolch	*Tepee Stories*	Garrard
2	3-9	Dolch	*"Why" Stories*	Garrard
2	2-6	Dolch	*Wigwam Stories*	Garrard
2	3-4	Eager	*Red Head*	Hale
2	2-4	Elkin	*The Big Jump and Other Stories*	Random
2	3-4	Fatio	*The Happy Lion*	McGraw
2	3-4	Fatio	*The Happy Lion Roars*	McGraw
2	3-4	Flack	*Boats on the River*	Viking
2	2-8	Ford	*Davy Crockett*	Putnam
2	2-0	Friedman	*Ben Franklin*	Putnam
2	1-4	Friedman	*Boy Who Lived in a Cave*	Putnam
2	3-4	Gag	*Millions of Cats*	Coward
2	3-4	Gannett	*Elmer and the Dragon*	Random
2	2-4	Gans	*It's Nesting Time*	Crowell
2	2-6	Gates	*Buster the Burro*	Macmillan
2	2-5	Gates	*It Is a Big Country*	Macmillan
2	2-6	Gates	*On a Tugboat*	Macmillan
2	2-5	Gates	*The Princess with the Dirty Face*	Macmillan
2	2-6	Gates	*Skippy the Monkey*	Macmillan
2	3-4	Gilbert	*Mr. Plum and the Little Green Tree*	Abingdon
2	3-4	Goudey	*Here Come the Bears*	Scribner
2	3-4	Goudey	*Here Come the Beavers*	Scribner
2	3-4	Goudey	*Here Come the Elephants*	Scribner
2	2-6	Hader	*Farmer in the Dell*	Macmillan
2	3-4	Hader	*Home on the Range*	Macmillan
2	1-4	Hader	*The Mighty Hunter*	Macmillan
2	2-5	Hildreth	*The Story Road*	Holt
2	2-5	Hildreth	*Along the Way*	Holt
2	2-6	Hoban	*Tom and the Two Handles*	Harper
2	1-4	Hoff	*Danny and the Dinosaur*	Harper
2	1-4	Hoff	*Sammy the Seal*	Harper
2	3-9	Hogner	*Spiders*	Crowell
2	3-4	Huber	*After the Sun Sets*	Harper
2	1-5	Huber, et al.	*It Happened One Day*	Harper

2	3-4	Ipcar	*World Full of Horses*	Doubleday
2	3-4	Kahl	*Away Went Wolfgang*	Scribner
2	3-4	Kahl	*The Duchess Bakes a Cake*	Scribner
2	1-5	King	*Mabel the Whale*	Follett
2	3-9	Kissin	*Desert Animals*	Hale
2	3-4	Krauss	*The Backward Day*	Harper
2-3	2-7	Kravetz	*A Horse of Another Color*	Little
2-3	1-4	Lenski	*Cowboy Small*	Walck
2	1-2	Lenski	*The Little Airplane*	Walck
2-3	1-4	Lenski	*Little Fire Engine*	Walck
2	3-9	Lent	*Straight Down*	Macmillan
2	K-5	Lewellen	*True Book of Airports and Airplanes*	Childrens
2	K-4	Lewellen	*True Book of Farm Animals*	Childrens
2	1-4	Liebers	*Stevie Finds a Way*	Abingdon
2	1-6	Lindop	*Jumbo, King of the Elephants*	Little
2-3	2-5	Martin	*The Little Brown Hen*	Crowell
2	2-5	Martin	*Pocahontas*	Putnam
2	1-5	Martin	*The Raccoon and Mrs. McGinnes*	Putnam
2	2-5	Martini	*True Book of Indians*	Childrens
2	1-5	McCall	*The Buttons Go Camping*	Benefic
2	2-5	McClung	*Possum*	Morrow
2	3-4	McGinley	*The Horse Who Lived Upstairs*	Lippincott
2-3	2-6	Miles	*Mississippi Possum*	Little
2	1-5	Moore	*Old Rosie—the Horse Nobody Understood*	Random
2-3	3-8	Norman	*Johnny Appleseed*	Putnam
2	2-4	Olds	*Miss Hattie and the Monkey*	Follett
2-3	2-7	Pine	*Air All Around*	McGraw
2	K-5	Podendorf	*True Book of Animal Homes*	Childrens
2-3	2-5	Podendorf	*True Book of Spiders*	Childrens
2	3-4	Pratt and Meighen	*Story Train*	Singer
2	2-8	Quigg	*Jenny Jones and Skid*	Walck
2	1-4	Renick	*Boy at Bat*	Scribner
2-3	1-4	Schwartz	*When Animals are Babies*	Holiday
2	2-6	Scott	*Molly and the Tool Shed*	Harcourt
2	2-4	Selsam	*Greg's Microscope*	Harper
2	2-4	Selsam	*Let's Get Turtles*	Harper
2	2-4	Selsam	*Plenty of Fish*	Harper
2	2-4	Selsam	*Terry and the Caterpillars*	Harper
2	1-5	Sharp, et al.	*Little Lost Bobo*	Steck
2	2-6	Sharp and Young	*Rainbow in the Sky*	Steck
2-3	2-5	Showers	*Your Skin and Mine*	Crowell
2	3-4	Simont	*Polly's Oats*	Hale
2-3	1-6	Slobodkina	*Caps for Sale*	Scott, W. R.
2	3-4	Slobodkina	*The Seaweed Hat*	Hale
2	3-4	Smith	*Down the Road with Johnny*	Hale
2	1-4	Thayer	*The Outside Cat*	Morrow
2	3-4	Tippett	*Tools for Andy*	Hale
2	3-4	Tresselt	*Autumn Harvest*	Lathrop
2	3-4	Tresselt	*Sun Up*	Lathrop

2	3-4	Tresselt	*Hi, Mister Robin*	Lathrop
2-3	1-5	Voight	*Patch, A Baby Mink*	Putnam
2	2-8	Walters	*The Steam Shovel that Wouldn't Eat Dirt*	Dutton
2	2-5	Watson	*The Whale Hunt*	Golden
2	2-6	Will	*Circus Ruckus*	Harcourt
2	2-6	Will	*The Christmas Bunny*	Harcourt
2	3-4	Woolley	*I Like Trains*	Harper
2	2-4	Ziner	*The True Book of Time*	Childrens

Grade 3

READING LEVEL	INTEREST LEVEL	AUTHOR	TITLE	PUBLISHER
3	4-9	Adrian	*Honeybee*	Holiday
3-4	2-6	Adrian	*Gray Squirrel*	Holiday
3-4	2-6	Aesop	*Aesop's Fables (Harris, Ed.)*	Doubleday
3-4	3-6	Agle and Wilson	*Three Boys and a Helicopter*	Scribner
3	3-8	Agle and Wilson	*Three Boys and a Lighthouse*	Scribner
3	3-8	Allen	*Tammy Chipmunk and His Friends*	Houghton
3	3-8	Allen	*Everyday Birds*	Houghton
3	3-6	Anderson	*Pilot Jack Knight*	Harper
3	4-5	Anderson	*A Pony for Linda*	Macmillan
3	1-6	Anderson	*Blaze and the Gypsies*	Macmillan
3	2-5	Anderson	*Blaze and the Mountain Lion*	Macmillan
3	1-6	Anderson	*Blaze Finds the Trail*	Macmillan
3	1-6	Anderson	*Blaze and the Forest Fire*	Macmillan
3	1-6	Anderson	*Billy and Blaze*	Macmillan
3	1-6	Anderson	*Blaze and Thunderbolt*	Macmillan
3	3-10	Anderson	*Alec Majors*	Harper
3	3-10	Anderson	*Friday, the Arapaho Indian*	Harper
3	3-8	Anderson	*Portugee Phillips and the Fighting Sioux*	Harper
3	4-9	Anderson	*Linda and the Indians*	Macmillan
3	3-10	Anderson	*Squanto and the Pilgrims*	Harper
3	4-9	Antonacci	*Baseball for Young Champions*	McGraw
3	4-5	Ardizzone	*Little Tim and the Brave Sea Captain*	Walck
3	4-5	Ardizzone	*Tim to the Rescue*	Walck
3	4-5	Ardizzone	*Tim All Alone*	Walck
3-4	1-7	Aulaire	*Abraham Lincoln*	Doubleday
3-4	1-7	Aulaire	*George Washington*	Doubleday
3	4-9	Baldwin	*Favorite Tales of Long Ago*	Dutton
3	3-6	Ballard	*True Book of Reptiles*	Childrens
3	4-5	Bannon	*Billy and the Bear*	Houghton
3	4-5	Barnet	*Stories of Fun*	Macmillan
3	4-5	Barnet	*Mrs. Talky and Jim Spot*	Macmillan
3	2-7	Barnum	*The New Fire Engine*	Morrow
3	2-5	Barr	*Texas Pete*	Whitman
3	4-9	Beals	*Chief Black Hawk*	Harper
3	4-5	Beatty	*Little Wild Horse*	Houghton
3	2-6	Beatty	*Little Owl Indian*	Houghton

3	4-9	Beim	*Flood Waters*	Harcourt
3	4-9	Beim	*Country Garage*	Morrow
3	4-5	Beim	*Kid Brother*	Morrow
3	4-5	Beim	*Smallest Boy in the Class*	Morrow
3-4	2-6	Belting	*The Long-Tailed Bear and Other Indian Legends*	Bobbs
3	4-5	Bemelmans	*Madeline and the Bad Hat*	Viking
3	4-9	Bendick	*What Could You See?*	McGraw
3	4-12	Berres	*Submarine Rescue*	Harr
3	4-12	Berres	*The Pearl Divers*	Harr
3	4-12	Berres	*Frogmen in Action*	Harr
3	3-8	Bishop	*Five Chinese Brothers*	Hale
3	2-6	Black	*Dusty and His Friends*	Holiday
3-4	2-7	Blough	*Bird Watchers and Bird Feeders*	McGraw
3-4	3-9	Bontemps	*The Fast Sooner Hound*	Houghton
3	3-8	Bothwell	*Little Boat Boy*	Harcourt
3-4	3-6	Brenner	*A Bird in the Family*	Scott
3	4-9	Brewster	*First Book of Baseball*	Watts
3	4-9	Bridges	*Zoo Pets*	Morrow
3-4	3-6	Brock	*The Plaid Cow*	Knopf
3	2-6	Bronson	*Hooker's Holiday*	Harcourt
3	3-8	Bronson	*Coyotes*	Harcourt
3	4-5	Brooks	*Freddy Goes to Florida*	Knopf
3	4-9	Brown	*Little Pig's Picnic*	Heath
3	4-5	Buck	*In Yards and Gardens*	Abingdon
3	4-5	Buff	*Apple and the Arrow*	Houghton
3	4-9	Bulla	*Ghost Town Treasure*	Crowell
3	4-9	Bulla	*Star of Wild Horse Canyon*	Crowell
3	2-5	Bulla	*The Poppy Seeds*	Crowell
3	4-9	Bulla	*Pirates Promise*	Hale
3	3-5	Bulla	*The Valentine Cat*	Crowell
3-4	4-10	Bulla	*Viking Adventure*	Crowell
3	3-6	Bulla	*John Billington, Friend of Squanto*	Crowell
3	4-9	Bulla	*The Sword in the Tree*	Crowell
3	4-9	Burton	*Mike Mulligan and His Steam Shovel*	Houghton
3	4-9	Burton	*Katy and the Big Snow*	Houghton
3	3-8	Butterfield	*Morning Star*	(Lyons) Meredith
3	3-8	Butterfield	*Little Wind*	(Lyons) Meredith
3	3-6	Calhoun	*Cowboy Cal and the Outlaw*	Morrow
3	2-5	Carlisle	*The True Book of Automobiles*	Childrens
3	3-6	Carona	*The True Book of Numbers*	Childrens
3	4-5	Carroll	*Tough Enough*	Walck
3	4-5	Carroll	*Tough Enough's Pony*	Walck
3	4-5	Carroll	*Beanie*	Walck
3	3-8	Carson	*Peter and the Two-Hour Moon*	Benefic
3	3-8	Carson	*Peter and the Rocket Ship*	Benefic
3-4	3-12	Cary	*Meet Abraham Lincoln*	Random
3	3-6	Chandler	*Charley Brave*	Whitman
3	2-9	Chandler	*Cowboy Sam and the Rustlers*	Benefic
3	2-9	Chandler	*Cowboy Sam and the Indians*	Benefic
3	3-8	Chandler	*Little Wolf and the Thunder Stick*	Benefic

3-4	4-8	Christopher	*Basketball Sparkplug*	Little
3	3-4	Christopher	*Baseball Pals*	Little
3	2-5	Ciardi	*I Met a Man*	Houghton
3	4-5	Clark	*Blue Canyon Horse*	Viking
3	4-5	Coatsworth	*Away Goes Sally*	Macmillan
3	4-5	Coatsworth	*First Adventure*	Macmillan
3	3-5	Coatsworth	*You Say You Saw a Camel?*	Harper
3	4-5	Coatsworth	*The Sod House*	Macmillan
3	4-9	Colby	*Leatherneck*	Coward
3	4-5	Colby	*Gabbit, the Magic Rabbit*	Hale
3-4	3-9	Colver	*Abraham Lincoln*	Garrard
3-4	3-12	Corbett	*What Makes a Car Go?*	Little
3	4-9	Credle	*Down, Down the Mountain*	Nelsen
3	4-5	Credle	*Flop-Eared Hound*	Hale
3	4-5	Creekmore	*Fujio*	Macmillan
3	3-6	Crosby	*Junior Science Book of Beavers*	Grosset
3-4	3-12	Crosby	*Junior Science Book of Stars*	Grosset
3	4-9	Dalgliesh	*Fourth of July Story*	Scribner
3	4-9	Dalgliesh	*America Begins*	Scribner
3	3-6	Dalgliesh	*The Bears on Hemlock Mountain*	Scribner
3	3-5	Dalgliesh	*The Columbus Story*	Scribner
3	4-9	Dalgliesh	*Thanksgiving Story*	Scribner
3	4-5	Dalgliesh	*America Travels*	Macmillan
3	2-7	Daugherty	*Andy and the Lion*	Viking
3	3-7	Davis	*Roger and the Fox*	Doubleday
3	4-5	DeJong	*Smoke Above the Lane*	Harper
3	1-5	Dennis	*Flip and the Cows*	Viking
3	1-5	Dennis	*Flip*	Viking
3	4-5	Dobbs	*Once Upon a Time*	Random
3-4	3-9	Dobler	*Cyrus McCormick: Farmer Boy*	Bobbs
3	2-9	Dolch	*Aesop's Stories*	Garrard
3	2-9	Dolch	*Bible Stories*	Garrard
3	2-6	Dolch	*Fairy Stories*	Garrard
3	2-9	Dolch	*Famous Stories*	Garrard
3	2-9	Dolch	*Far East Stories*	Garrard
3	2-9	Dolch	*Gospel Stories*	Garrard
3	2-9	Dolch	*Greek Stories*	Garrard
3	2-5	DuBois	*Otto in Africa*	Viking
3	2-6	DuBois	*Otto in Texas*	Viking
3	4-9	Duvoisin	*Petunia*	Knopf
3	4-9	Eisner	*Buried Gold*	Follett
3	4-9	Eisner	*Mystery of Broken Wheel Ranch*	Follett
3	1-5	Elkin	*Six Foolish Fishermen*	Hale
3	2-5	Elkin	*Lucky and the Giant*	Childrens
3-4	2-6	Epstein	*Spring Holidays*	Garrard
3	4-5	Erickson	*Slip, the Story of a Little Fox*	Hale
3-4	3-7	Evans	*A Camel in the Tent*	Whitman, Albert
3-4	3-5	Evans	*One Good Deed Deserves Another*	Whitman, Albert
3	3-5	Farquhar	*Indian Children of America*	Holt
3	3-9	Faulkner	*Hidden Silver*	Scott, Foresman
3	4-5	**Gag**	*Tales from Grimm*	Hale

3	3-7	Gates	*Robin Fly South*	Macmillan
3	3-6	Gates	*A Cat Becomes Contented*	Macmillan
3	3-7	Gates	*Good Times Together*	Macmillan
3	3-6	Gates	*Kurti and Hardi*	Macmillan
3	2-6	Gates	*True Book of Conversation*	Childrens
3	3-7	Gates	*Susan and the Sheep*	Macmillan
3	3-6	Gates	*The Sad Prince*	Macmillan
3	1-8	Seuss	*Horton Hatches the Egg*	Random
3	3-8	Gifford	*Red Feather's Adventure*	Lyons
3-4	3-5	Goudey	*Here Come the Deer!*	Scribner
3-4	3-5	Goudey	*Here Come the Raccoons!*	Scribner
3-4	3-12	Graff	*George Washington*	Garrard
3	3-9	Graff	*Squanto: Indian Adventurer*	Garrard
3	3-8	Graham	*Timothy Turtle*	Viking
3	3-4	Gramatky	*Little Toot*	Hale
3	3-4	Gramatky	*Loopy*	Hale
3	2-9	Graves	*Benjamin Franklin*	Garrard
3-4	3-9	Graves	*John F. Kennedy: New Frontiersman*	Garrard
3	3-6	Hader	*Pancho*	Macmillan
3	2-7	Haywood	*Eddie and Gardenia*	Morrow
3	3-8	Haywood	*Primrose Day*	Harcourt
3-4	3-6	Haywood	*Eddie and Louella*	Morrow
3	2-6	Haywood	*Eddie and the Fire Engine*	Morrow
3	2-6	Haywood	*Betsy's Little Star*	Morrow
3-4	3-7	Henry	*Five O'Clock Charlie*	Rand
3	1-6	Hildreth	*Faraway Ports*	Holt
3	1-6	Hildreth	*Enchanting Stories*	Holt
3	3-6	Hinshaw	*True Book of Your Body and You*	Childrens
3-4	3-6	Holland	*Teddy's Camp-Out*	Knopf
3	4-5	Holt	*Lance and Cowboy Billy*	McGraw
3	2-6	Hornblow	*Animals Do the Strangest Things*	Random
3	4-5	Huber, et al.	*After the Sun Sets*	Harper
3	4-5	Huntington	*Let's Go to the Seashore*	Doubleday
3	4-5	Huntington	*Let's Go to the Brook*	Doubleday
3	4-5	Huntington	*Let's Go to the Desert*	Doubleday
3	4-9	Jackson	*Spice's Football*	Crowell
3	4-5	Johnson	*The Treat Shop*	Merrill
3	3-5	Johnson	*Jamie, a Basset Hound*	Morrow
3	4-9	Kottmeyer	*King Arthur and His Knights*	McGraw
3	3-10	Kottmeyer	*The Robin Hood Stories*	McGraw
3	4-10	Kottmeyer	*The Trojan War*	McGraw
3-4	3-8	Krasilovsky	*Benny's Flag*	World
3	2-6	Krauss	*A Good Man and His Good Wife*	Harper
3-4	2-7	Larom	*Bronco Charlie: Rider of the Pony Express*	McGraw
3	1-5	Lasson	*Which Witch?*	McKay
3	4-5	Lawson	*Edward, Hoppy and Joe*	Hale
3	1-7	Leaf	*Story of Ferdinand*	Viking
3	2-5	Lindop	*Pelorus Jack: Dolphin Pilot*	Little
3	3-6	McCall	*Buttons at the Soap Box Derby*	Benefic
3	4-5	McClung	*Stripe: The Story of a Chipmunk*	Morrow

3-4	3-6	McClung	*Mammals and How They Live*	Random
3	4-5	McClung	*Major: The Story of a Black Bear*	Morrow
3	4-5	McClung	*Spike: The Story of a Whitetail Deer*	Morrow
3-4	3-9	Machetanz	*Robbie and the Sled Dog Race*	Scribner
3	4-5	Mason	*The Middle Sister*	Macmillan
3-4	3-8	Mason	*Kate Douglas Wiggin: The Little Schoolteacher*	Bobbs
3	4-5	Mason	*Hominy and His Blunt-Nosed Arrow*	Macmillan
3	4-5	Mason	*Pony Called Lightning*	Macmillan
3	3-6	Mason	*The Gray-Nosed Kitten*	Houghton
3	3-6	Moon	*One Little Indian*	Whitman, Albert
3	4-5	Moore	*Old Rosie—The Horse Nobody Understood*	Random
3	4-9	Morrison	*Black Within and Red Without: A Book of Riddles*	Crowell
3	4-5	Obermeyer	*The Six Robbins*	Scott
3	4-5	Palmer	*Mickey Never Fails*	Heath
3-4	2-7	Podendorf	*True Book of Rocks and Minerals*	Childrens
3	3-6	Podendorf	*True Book of Plant Experiments*	Childrens
3	3-6	Rabe	*United Nations Day*	Crowell
3	1-6	Rey	*Curious George Takes a Job*	Houghton
3	4-5	Rey	*Curious George*	Houghton
3	4-5	Rey	*Curious George Flies a Kite*	Houghton
3	4-5	Rey	*Curious George Rides a Bike*	Houghton
3	2-7	Robinson	*Buttons*	Viking
3-4	3-9	Russell	*Sugaring Time*	Abingdon
3	4-5	Schneider	*Let's Find Out*	Scott, W. R.
3	3-8	Schneider	*How Big is Big?*	Hale
3	4-5	Schneider	*Now Try This*	Hale
3	4-5	Schneider	*While Susie Sleeps*	Scott, W. R.
3	3-6	Scott	*Judy's Baby*	Harcourt
3	3-6	Scott	*Benjie and His Family*	Harcourt
3	1-8	Scott	*Mr. Doodle*	Harcourt
3	4-5	Selsam	*See Through the Forest*	Harper
3	4-5	Selsam	*See Through the Lake*	Harper
3	4-5	Selsam	*See Through the Sea*	Harper
3	4-5	Seuss	*Horton Hatches a Who*	Random
3	4-5	Seuss	*Horton Hatches the Egg*	Harper
3	1-6	Seuss	*And to Think I Saw It on Mulberry Street*	Vanguard
3-4	3-6	Seuss	*Dr. Yertle the Turtle and Other Stories*	Random
3	4-5	Seuss	*How the Grinch Stole Christmas*	Random
3	3-8	Sharp and Young	*Whatnot Tales*	Steck
3	1-5	Sharp	*Chippy Chipmunk's Vacation*	Steck
3	4-9	Slaughter	*Horses Around the World*	Lippincott
3	4-5	Slobodkina	*Magic Michael*	Macmillan
3	2-8	Slobodkina	*Dinny and Danny*	Macmillan
3-4	2-7	Snow	*Sequoyah: Young Cherokee Guide*	Bobbs

3	4-10	Kottmeyer	*Greek and Roman Myths*	McGraw
3	3-6	Swift	*Little Red Lighthouse and the Great Gray Bridge*	Harcourt
3	3-5	Tooze	*Silver From the Sea*	Viking
3-4	3-6	Vance	*Windows for Rosemary*	Dutton
3	3-8	Voight	*Nathan Hale*	Putnam
3	4-5	Ward	*The Biggest Bear*	Houghton
3	3-9	Warner	*Yellow House Mystery*	Scott, Foresman
3	4-9	Warner	*The Boxcar Children*	Scott, Foresman
3	4-9	Warner	*Surprise Island*	Scott, Foresman
3	2-8	Warner	*1001 Nights*	Scott, Foresman
3	3-5	Watson	*Sugar on Snow*	Viking
3	4-5	Webb	*Song of the Seasons*	Morrow
3	4-5	Yashima	*Crow Boy*	Viking
3	4-5	Yashima	*The Village Tree*	Viking
3	4-5	Yashima	*Plenty to Watch*	Viking
3	2-5	Zimmerman	*Corky in Orbit*	Reilly
3	2-4	Zion	*Harry and the Lady Next Door*	Harper
3	4-5	Zoff	*Riddles Around the World*	Pantheon

Grade 4

READING LEVEL	INTEREST LEVEL	AUTHOR	TITLE	PUBLISHER
4	3-7	Agle	*Three Boys and the Remarkable Cow*	Scribner
4	5-9	Anderson	*Marmaduke*	Gilbert
4	5-6	Angelo	*Big Little Island*	Viking
4-5	4-9	Antonacci	*Basketball for Young Champions*	McGraw
4	4-8	Atwater	*Mr. Popper's Penguins*	Little
4	4-8	Averill	*Daniel Boone*	Harper
4	5-9	Bailey	*The Little Red*	Viking
4	3-9	Bare	*John Deere: Blacksmith Boy*	Bobbs
4	5-9	Batchelor	*Communication: from Cave Writing to Television*	Harcourt
4	4-10	Beals	*Chief Black Hawk*	Harper
4	4-12	Beals	*Dan Morgan—Rifleman*	Harper
4	4-12	Beals	*Kit Carson*	Harper
4	4-10	Beals	*The Story of Robinson Crusoe*	Sanborn
4	5-6	Beim	*Beach Boy*	Harcourt
4	2-6	Beim	*B'ue Jeans*	Harcourt
4	5-6	Bennett	*Little Witch*	Lippincott
4	4-9	Berglund	*Tom Sawyer*	Scott, Foresman
4	5-9	Bernhard	*Wonders of the World*	Golden
4	4-8	Best	*Desmond's First Case*	Viking
4	5-9	Biermiller	*Starboy*	Holt
4	4-7	Biestervold	*Run, Reddy, Run*	Nelson
4	5-9	Bishop	*Pancakes—Paris*	Viking

4	5-6	Blanck	*The King and the Noble Blacksmith*	Hale
4	5-9	Blough	*When You Go to the Zoo*	McGraw
4-5	4-9	Bonner	*Two-Way Pitcher*	Lantern
4	5-6	Bontemps	*The Fast Sooner Hound*	Houghton
4	5-6	Bontemps	*Sam Patch, the High, Wide and Handsome Jumper*	Hale
4	4-8	Borland	*Allan Pinkerton: Young Detective*	Bobbs
4	4-12	Borten	*Halloween*	Crowell
4	5-9	Bradley	*Cappy and the Jet Engine*	Lippincott
4	4-7	Branley	*A Book of Satellites for You*	Crowell
4	4-12	Brewster	*The First Book of Baseball*	Watts
4	5-6	Brink	*Family Sabbatical*	Viking
4	5-9	Brock	*Here Comes Kristie*	Knopf
4	4-8	Broderick	*Training a Companion Dog*	Prentice
4	2-6	Bronson	*Cats*	Harcourt
4	5-6	Bronson	*Pinto's Journey*	Messner
4	4-9	Brown	*Huckleberry Finn*	Scott, Foresman
4	4-12	Brown and Moderow	*The Last of the Mohicans*	Scott, Foresman
4	5-12	Brown	*Moby Dick*	Scott, Foresman
4	3-8	Bulla	*The Secret Valley*	Crowell
4	3-8	Bulla	*Surprise for a Cowboy*	Crowell
4	3-6	Bulla	*Ranch for Danny*	Crowell
4	3-8	Bulla	*Riding the Pony Express*	Crowell
4	5-6	Bunce	*Freight Train*	Putnam
4	5-12	Bunce	*Prince and the Pauper*	Scott, Foresman
4	5-9	Cameron	*Wonderful Flight to the Mushroom Planet*	Little
4	5-9	Cameron	*Stowaway to the Mushroom Planet*	Little
4	5-6	Carlson	*Alphonse, That Bearded One*	Harcourt
4-5	4-10	Carlson	*The Empty Schoolhouse*	Harper
4	5-6	Carlson	*The Family Under the Bridge*	Harper
4	5-9	Cavanah	*Our Country's Story*	Hale
4	5-6	Chase	*Grandfather Tales*	Houghton
4	5-6	Chase	*Jack and the Three Sillies*	Houghton
4	4-12	Christopher	*Counterfeit Tackle*	Little
4	4-8	Christopher	*Tall Man in the Pivot*	Little
4	5-6	Cleary	*Ellen Tebbits*	Morrow
4	5-6	Cleary	*Henry Huggins*	Morrow
4	5-6	Cleary	*Henry and Beezus*	Morrow
4	5-6	Cleary	*Henry and the Paper Route*	Morrow
4	4-7	Cleary	*Ribsy*	Morrow
4	4-12	Clymer	*Wheels*	Holt
4	3-7	Coates	*The Sign of the Open Hand*	Scribner
4-5	4-7	Coatsworth	*Desert Dan*	Viking
4	5-6	Coblentz	*Martin and Abraham Lincoln*	Grosset
4	5-6	Cochrane	*Let's Go to the United Nations Headquarters*	Putnam

4-5	4-7	Corbett	*The Mailbox Trick*	Little
4	4-12	Corbett	*What Makes TV Work?*	Little
4	5-9	Corbett	*Susie Sneakers*	Crowell
4	4-6	Courtney	*What Does a Barometer Do?*	Little
4-5	4-9	Dalgliesh	*America Begins*	Scribner
4	5-9	Dalgliesh	*The Columbus Story*	Scribner
4	5-9	Dalgliesh	*The Bears on Hemlock Mountain*	Scribner
4-5	4-8	Dalgliesh	*The Fourth of July Story*	Scribner
4	5-9	Dalgliesh	*Ride on the Wind*	Scribner
4-5	4-12	David	*Spiders and How They Live*	Prentice
4	4-8	De Angeli	*Jared's Islands*	Doubleday
4	5-6	Dennis	*Flip*	Viking
4	5-6	Dennis	*Flip and the Cows*	Viking
4	5-6	Dennis	*Flip and the Morning*	Viking
4	5-12	Dickens	*A Tale of Two Cities* (adapted)	McGraw
4	3-7	DuBois	*The Alligator Case*	Harper
4	5-6	Duvoisin	*They Put Out to Sea*	Knopf
4	4-10	Edmonds	*Two Logs Crossing*	Dodd
4	5-6	Enright	*Gone-Away-Lake*	Harcourt
4	5-6	Enright	*The Saturdays*	Holt
4	5-6	Enright	*Four-Story Mistake*	Holt
4	5-6	Enright	*Then There Were Five*	Holt
4	5-6	Enright	*Spiderweb for Two*	Holt
4	5-9	Estes	*Ginger Pye*	Harcourt
4	5-9	Estes	*Pinkey Pye*	Harcourt
4	5-6	Ets	*Oley: The Sea Monster*	Viking
4	5-8	Evans	*People Are Important*	Capitol
4	5-9	Evans	*Why We Live Where We Live*	Little
4-5	4-6	Faber	*The Life of Pocahontas*	Prentice
4	4-7	Fenton	*The Moon for Young Explorers*	Day
4	5-9	Fenton	*Prehistoric World*	Day
4	5-9	Fisher	*You and the United Nations*	Childrens
4	4-9	Foltz	*Awani*	Morrow
4-5	4-8	Foltz	*Tuchin's Mayan Treasure*	Morrow
4	5-9	Freeman	*Fun with Astronomy*	Random
4	4-8	Freeman	*Fun with Cooking*	Random
4-5	4-12	Freschet	*Young Eagle*	Scribner
4	5-6	Fritz	*The Cabin Faced West*	Coward
4	5-6	Frost	*Windy Foot at the County Fair*	McGraw
4	5-6	Frost	*Sleighbells for Windy Foot*	McGraw
4	5-6	Frost	*Maple Sugar for Windy Foot*	McGraw
4	5-12	Gallant	*Exploring Mars*	Garden
4	5-6	Gannett	*My Father's Dragon*	Random
4	4-12	Garst	*Cowboy and Cattle Trails*	Harper
4	4-7	Gates	*Sharing More Adventures*	Macmillan
4	3-8	Geisel	*500 Hats of Bartholomew Cubbins*	Hale
4	3-8	Geisel	*McElligot's Pool*	Randon
4	4-9	George	*Snow Tracks*	Dutton
4-5	4-9	Goetz	*The Artic Tundra*	Morrow
4	4-10	Goetz	*Swamps*	Morrow
4-5	3-6	Goudey	*Here Come the Dolphins!*	Scribner
4	3-8	Gramatky	*Hercules*	Putnam
4	3-7	Gray	*Just Imagine*	Scott, Foresman

4	4-10	Guilfoyle	*A Holiday Book: Valentine's Day*	Garrard
4	3-6	Hader	*Reindeer Trail*	Macmillan
4	4-8	Hamilton	*Let's Go Aboard An Automatic Submarine*	Putnam
4-5	4-7	Harnden	*Golly and the Gulls*	Houghton
4-5	4-8	Hawkinson	*Collect, Print and Paint from Nature*	Whitman
4	3-6	Hays	*The Little Horse that Raced the Train*	Little
4	3-6	Hays	*Pilgrim Thanksgiving*	Coward
4	5-6	Haywood	*B is for Betsy*	Harcourt
4	2-6	Haywood	*Betsy and Billy*	Harcourt
4	5-6	Haywood	*Little Eddie*	Morrow
4	5-6	Haywood	*Eddie and the Fire Engine*	Morrow
4	2-6	Haywood	*Here's a Penny*	Harcourt
4	2-6	Haywood	*Penny and Peter*	Harcourt
4	4-12	Heffernan, *et al.*	*Desert Treasure*	Harr
4	5-9	Heffernan	*The Mysterious Swamp Rider*	Harr
4	5-6	Heppner	*Inki*	Macmillan
4-5	4-7	Hicks	*First Boy on the Moon*	Holt
4	5-12	Hinton	*Exploring Under the Sea*	Doubleday
4-5	4-9	Hitte	*Hurricanes, Tornadoes, and Blizzards*	Random
4	5-9	Hoff	*Johnny Texas on the San Antonio Road*	Follett
4	5-9	Hoff	*Johnny Texas*	Follett
4	4-8	Huber	*It Must be Magic*	Harper
4	5-6	Hunt	*Ladycake Farm*	Lippincott
4	5-6	Hunt	*Stars for Christy*	Lippincott
4	5-6	Hunt	*Christy at Skippinghills*	Lippincott
4-5	4-8	Hunter	*Child of the Silent Night*	Houghton
4	5-6	Huntington	*Let's Go to the Brook*	Doubleday
4	5-9	Johnson	*Larry of Snow Ridge*	Morrow
4	4-8	Johnson and Jacobs	*Magic Carpet*	Merrill
4	6-12	Jordan, *et al.*	*Lorna Doone*	Scott, Foresman
4	5-12	Judson	*Benjamin Franklin*	Follett
4	4-7	Justus	*Lester and His Hound Pup*	Hastings
4-5	3-8	Kay	*Lincoln: A Big Man*	Hastings
4	5-9	Kettelkamp	*Magic Made Easy*	Morrow
4	5-9	Kettelkamp	*The Magic of Sound*	Morrow
4	6-12	Kottmeyer	*Ben Hur*	McGraw
4	4-12	Kottmeyer	*Cases of Sherlock Holmes*	McGraw
4	4-10	Kottmeyer	*The Flamingo Feather*	McGraw
4	5-12	Kottmeyer	*The Gold Bug and Other Stories*	McGraw
4	4-12	Kottmeyer	*To Have and to Hold*	McGraw
4	7-12	Kottmeyer	*Ivanhoe*	McGraw
4	6-12	Kottmeyer	*Juarez, Hero of Mexico*	McGraw
4	4-10	Kottmeyer	*Men of Iron*	McGraw
4	5-9	Lansing	*Deep River Raft*	Crowell
4	5-9	Lathrop	*Let Them Live*	Macmillan

4	5-9	Lauber	*Clarence, the TV Dog*	Coward
4	4-10	Lauber	*Junior Science Book of Penguins*	Garrard
4-5	4-12	Leach	*Noodles, Nitwits and Numbskills*	World
4	5-6	Leach	*The Turnspit Dog*	Hale
4	5-9	Leaf	*The Story of Ferdinand*	Viking
4-5	3-9	LeGrand	*How Baseball Began in Brooklyn*	Abingdon
4-5	3-9	LeGrand	*How Space Rockets Began*	Abingdon
4	5-9	LeGrand	*Matilda*	Abingdon
4	5-9	Lenski	*Boom Town Boy*	Lippincott
4	5-12	Lewellen	*Helicopters: How They Work*	Crowell
4	5-12	Lewellen	*Earth Satellite*	Knopf
4	5-12	Lewis	*Stamp Collecting*	Knopf
4	5-6	Lindgren	*Pippi Lonstocking*	Viking
4	5	Lindgren	*Pippi Goes on Board*	Viking
4	5-6	Lindquist	*Golden Name Day*	Harper
4	5-9	Lyons	*Bluegrass Champion*	Grossett
4	4-5	McCloskey	*Lentil*	Viking
4	4-8	McClung	*Luna: The Story of a Moth*	Morrow
4	3-6	McClung	*Otus: The Story of a Screech Owl*	Morrow
4	5-6	McGinley	*The Plain Princess*	Lippincott
4	5-9	MacGregor	*Miss Pickerell Goes to Mars*	McGraw
4	5-9	MacGregor	*Miss Pickerell and the Geiger Counter*	McGraw
4	5-9	McNeer	*The California Gold Rush*	Random
4	3-8	Mason	*The Middle Sister*	Macmillan
4	4-6	Mason	*Steve and His Seven Orphans*	Houghton
4	4-9	Meadow-croft	*On Indian Trails with Daniel Boone*	Crowell
4	4-9	Meadow-croft	*Silver for General Washington*	Crowell
4	5-10	Moderow	*David Copperfield*	Scott, Foresman
4	5-12	Moderow	*Six Great Stories*	Scott, Foresman
4	4-10	Moderow	*Treasure Island*	Scott, Foresman
4	5-6	Moore	*The Snake that Went to School*	Random
4-5	4-8	Mowat	*Owls in the Family*	Little
4	4-9	Hill	*Robert Fulton and the Steamboat*	Random
4	5-6	Nash	*The Moon is Shining Bright As Day* (poems)	Lippincott
4	4-9	Neigoff	*Nine Makes a Team*	Whitman, Albert
4	5-6	Olds	*Feather Mountain*	Houghton
4	5-6	Parks	*Davy Crockett: Young Rifleman*	Bobbs
4	5-9	Patchett	*The Chance of Treasure*	Bobbs
4	4-7	Pearson	*The American Buffalo*	Steck
4	5-12	Peattie	*The Rainbow Book of Nature*	World
4	5-9	Pine	*The Indians Knew*	McGraw
4	5-12	Poe	*The Gold Bug and Other Stories* (adapted)	McGraw
4	6-10	Pulliam	*Rip Van Winkle and the Legend of Sleepy Hollow*	Steck

4	5-6	Rapaport	*Horse Chestnut Hideaway*	Putnam
4	4-8	Reid	*Mystery of the Carrowell Necklace*	Lathrop
4	3-7	Renick	*Nicky's Football Team*	Scribner
4	3-7	Renick	*Pete's Home Run*	Scribner
4	5-9	Renick	*The Dooleys Play Ball*	Scribner
4	5-9	Renick	*Touchdown for Doc*	Scribner
4	5-6	Rounds	*Ol' Paul, the Mighty Logger*	Hale
4	5-6	Rounds	*Whitey and the Blizzard*	Holiday
4	3-6	Rounds	*Whitey and the Colt-Killer*	Holiday
4	4-9	Sankey	*Basketballs for Breakfast*	Whitman, Albert
4	5-12	Scheele	*Prehistoric Animals*	World
4	5-9	Schneider	*Now Try This*	Hale
4	5-9	Schneider	*You Among the Stars*	Hale
4	5-9	Schneider	*How Your Body Works*	Scott, W. R.
4	4-12	Schneider	*Let's Find Out: A Picture Book of Science*	Scott, W. R.
4	5-9	Schneider	*Let's Look Under the City*	Scott, W. R.
4	5-9	Sears	*Firefly*	Holiday
4	5-12	Seibert	*Dan Beard: Boy Scout Pioneer*	Houghton
4	5-9	Selsam	*Play With Seeds*	Morrow
4	5-9	Seuss	*If I Ran the Zoo*	Random
4	5-9	Seuss	*If I Ran the Circus*	Random
4	5-9	Seuss	*Thidwick: The Big-Hearted Moose*	Random
4	5-9	Seuss	*McElligot's Pool*	Random
4	3-8	Sharp	*Gee Whillikins*	Steck
4	4-8	Sharp	*Gordo and the Hidden Treasure*	Steck
4	4-7	Sharp	*Simple Machines and How They Work*	Random
4	5-6	Shippen	*Lightfoot*	Viking
4	5-6	Slobodkin	*The Space Ship Under the Apple Tree*	Macmillan
4	5-6	Slobodkin	*The Space Ship Returns to the Apple Tree*	Macmillan
4-5	4-7	Sorensen	*Plain Girl*	Harcourt
4	5-9	Sorensen	*Miracles on Maple Hill*	Harcourt
4	7-12	Specking	*Simon Bolivar*	Webster
4	5-9	Steele	*Flaming Arrows*	Harcourt
4	5-9	Stevenson	*Abe Lincoln: Frontier Boy*	Bobbs
4	5-9	Stevenson	*Buffalo Bill: Boy of the Plains*	Bobbs
4	5-9	Stevenson	*Clara Barton: Girl Nurse*	Bobbs
4	5-9	Stuart	*Red Mule*	McGraw
4-5	4-10	Stuart	*The Rightful Owner*	Hale
4	4-12	Bendick	*The First Book of Automobiles*	Watts
4	3-8	Thorne	*East O' the Sun and West O' the Moon*	Harper
4	5-9	Todd	*Space Cat*	Scribner
4	5-9	Todd	*Space Cat Visits Venus*	Scribner
4	5-9	Todd	*Space Cat Meets Mars*	Scribner
4	4-12	Toles	*The Secret of Lonesome Valley*	Harr
4	5-9	Tousey	*Cowboy Tommy*	Hale

4	4-7	Tousey	*Davy Crockett, Hero of the Alamo*	Whitman, Albert
4	5-6	Watts	*Dozens of Cousins*	Hale
4	4-9	Weil	*Eleanor Roosevelt: Courageous Girl*	Bobbs
4	5-6	White	*Charlotte's Web*	Harper
4	5-9	White	*The Uninvited Donkey*	Viking
4-5	3-7	Wilder	*Little House in the Big Woods*	Hale
4	5-9	Wilder	*Little House on the Prairie*	Hale
4	4-12	Williamson	*The First Book of Bugs*	Watts
4	4-9	Wriston	*The Oom-Pah Horn*	Abingdon
4	5-9	Zim	*Comets*	Morrow
4	4-9	Zim	*Goldfish*	Morrow
4	5-9	Zim	*Snakes*	Morrow
4	4-9	Zim	*What's Inside of Plants*	Morrow
4	5-9	Zim	*Elephants*	Morrow

Grade 5

READING LEVEL	INTEREST LEVEL	AUTHOR	TITLE	PUBLISHER
5	4-9	Aardema	*Tales From the Story Hat*	Coward
5	6-9	Adams	*The Pony Express*	Random
5	6-9	Adams	*The Santa Fe Trail*	Random
5	4-9	Adler	*Why? A Book of Reasons*	Day
5	6-9	Anderson	*Fur Trappers of the Old West*	Harper
5	5-12	Anderson	*First Under the North Pole: The Voyage of the Nautilus*	World
5	4-9	Anderson	*Afraid to Ride*	Macmillan
5	6-9	Anderson	*Wild Bill Hickok*	Harper
5	6-9	Andrews	*All About Dinosaurs*	Random
5-6	5-9	Arundel	*Dugan and the Hobo*	McGraw
5	4-12	Baker	*Texas Yankee*	Harcourt
5	5-12	Baker	*Juan Ponce De Leon*	Knopf
5	6-9	Bartlett	*Insect Engineers, The Story of Ants*	Morrow
5	6-9	Beals	*Buffalo Bill*	Harper
5	6-9	Beals	*Chief Black Hawk*	Harper
5	6-9	Beals	*Davy Crockett*	Harper
5	6-9	Beals	*Kit Carson*	Harper
5	3-8	Beatty	*Matthew Looney's Voyage to Earth*	Scott, W. R.
5	6-12	Beeland	*Space Satellite*	Prentice
5	4-8	Beim	*Just Plain Maggie*	Harcourt
5	4-8	Beim	*Beach Boy*	Harcourt
5	6-9	Best	*Hay-Foot, Straw-Foot*	Viking
5	6-9	Bishop	*Twenty and Ten*	Viking
5	6-7	Blair	*Tall Tale America*	Coward
5	6-9	Bleeker	*The Apache Indians: Raiders of the Southwest*	Morrow
5	6-9	Bleeker	*The Cherokee: Indians of the Mountains*	Morrow
5	6-9	Bleeker	*The Chippewa Indians: Rice Gatherers of the Great Lakes*	Morrow

5	3-7	Blough	*Discovering Dinosaurs*	McGraw
5	3-8	Bialk	*The Horse Called Pete*	Houghton
5	4-9	Breetveld	*Getting to Know Alaska*	Coward
5	5-8	Brindze	*Story of Our Calendar*	Vanguard
5	6-9	Brink	*Caddie Woodlawn*	Macmillan
5	5-12	Bronowski	*Biography of an Atom*	Harper
5	6-9	Brown	*How to Make a Home Nature Museum*	Little
5	6-9	Brown	*How to Make a Miniature Zoo*	Little
5-6	5-12	Burchard	*Jed: The Story of a Yankee Soldier and a Southern Boy*	Coward
5	4-8	Burns	*To Be A Pioneer*	Abingdon
5	5-8	Burt	*Space Monkey*	Day
5-6	5-9	Butters	*The Bells of Freedom*	Macrae
5-6	5-12	Byrd	*The Black Wolf of Savage River*	Parnassus
5	5-12	Calhoun	*High Wind for Kansas*	Morrow
5	5-12	Carona	*Things That Measure*	Prentice
5	4-8	Carr	*Children of the Covered Wagon*	Crowell
5	6-9	Carter	*Mystery at Ding Dong Gulch*	Lippincott
5-6	4-10	Ceder	*Winter Without Salt*	Morrow
5	4-8	Chalmers	*Hundreds and Hundreds of Pancakes*	Viking
5	6-9	Chandler	*Too Many Promises*	Abelard
5	6-9	Clark	*Poppy Seed Cakes*	Doubleday
5	6-9	Clark	*The Dagger, the Fish, and Casey McKee*	McKay
5	6-9	Clark	*The River Showfolks*	McKay
5	6-9	Cleary	*Fifteen*	Morrow
5	5-10	Clewes	*The Mystery of the Midnight Smugglers*	Coward
5	6-12	Cloggins	*By Space Ship to the Moon*	Random
5	5-8	Coatsworth	*Thief Island*	Macmillan
5	6-9	Colby	*Park Rangers*	Coward
5-6	4-12	Collier	*The Story of Annie Oakley*	Grossett
5	6-10	Cone	*Only Jane*	Nelson
5	4-9	Coombs	*Project Mercury*	Morrow
5-6	5-12	Coombs	*Bush Flying in Alaska*	Morrow
5	4-12	Coombs	*Windows on the World*	World
5	5-9	Corbin	*Pony for Keeps*	Coward
5	5-12	Davis	*The Runaway Cattle*	Morrow
5	5-12	Davis	*Time of the Wolves*	Morrow
5	6-9	DeAngeli	*Bright April*	Doubleday
5	4-8	DeAngeli	*Bright Apple*	Doubleday
5	6-9	DeAngeli	*Thee, Hannah!*	Doubleday
5	6-9	DeAngeli	*Copper-Toed Boots*	Doubleday
5	5-8	De LaMare	*Mr. Bumps and His Monkey*	Holt
5	6-9	Dick	*Tornado's Big Year*	Wilcox
5	6-9	Dorian	*Trails West and the Men Who Made Them*	McGraw
5	6-12	Dumas	*The Three Musketeers* (adapted)	Sanborn
5	6-12	Dumas	*The Black Tulip* (adapted)	Longmans
5-6	4-9	Earle	*Camels and Llamas*	Morrow
5	6-12	Edmonds	*The Matchlock Gun*	Dodd
5	6-12	Earle	*Crickets*	Morrow

5	5-12	Edwards	*King Philip: Loyal Indian*	Houghton
5	5-10	Elting	*Spacecraft at Work*	Harvey
5	6-12	Engeman	*Annapolis: The Life Of A Midshipman*	Lathrop
5	6-12	Engeman	*The Coast Guard Academy*	Lathrop
5	6-12	Engeman	*West Point*	Lathrop
5	6-12	Engeman	*U.S. Air Force Academy*	Lathrop
5	6-9	Estes	*The Moffats*	Harcourt
5	6-9	Estes	*The Middle Moffat*	Harcourt
5	6-9	Estes	*Rufus M.*	Harcourt
5	4-7	Estes	*The Hundred Dresses*	Harcourt
5	5-12	Evans	*Written in Fire: The Story of Cattle Brands*	Holt
5-6	5-12	Felton	*William Phips and the Treasure Ship*	Dodd
5	6-9	Fenton	*The Golden Doors*	Doubleday
5	6-12	Canfield	*Understood Betsy*	Holt
5	4-8	Fisher	*Stories California Indians Told*	Hale
5	6-12	Foster	*George Washington*	Scribner
5	6-12	Foster	*Abraham Lincoln*	Scribner
5	5-12	Foster	*Andrew Jackson*	Scribner
5	4-7	Frankel	*Creating From Scrap*	Sterling
5	5-10	Freeman	*The Story of the Atom*	Random
5	5-9	Freeman	*The Story of Electricity*	Random
5	5-12	Friedman	*Ellen and the Gang*	Morrow
5	6-12	Friedman	*The Janitor's Girl*	Morrow
5	4-9	Fritz	*The Animals of Dr. Schweitzer*	Coward
5	6-12	Gallant	*Exploring the Moon*	Garden
5	6-12	Gallant	*Exploring the Planets*	Garden
5	6-12	Gallant	*Exploring the Weather*	Garden
5	6-9	Garst	*Cowboy Boots*	Abingdon
5	5-8	Gilbert	*Champions Don't Cry*	Harper
5	4-8	Goetz	*Deserts*	Morrow
5	6-9	Graham	*LaSalle, River Explorer*	Abingdon
5	5-12	Guy	*John Mosby: Rebel Raider of the Civil War*	Abelard
5	6-9	Hamid	*Boy Acrobat*	Sterling
5	4-8	Havighurst	*The First Book of Pioneers*	Watts
5	5-7	Hayes	*Project Genius*	Atheneum
5	5-12	Hays	*Pontiac: Lion in the Forest*	Houghton
5	6-9	Henry	*Black Gold*	Rand
5	6-9	Henry	*Misty of Chincoteague*	Rand
5	4-12	Hoban	*The Atomic Submarine*	Harper
5	6-9	Hofsinde	*Indian Sign Language*	Morrow
5	6-9	Holling	*Tree in the Trail*	Houghton
5	6-9	Holling	*Sea Bird*	Houghton
5	6-9	Holling	*Paddle-to-the-Sea*	Houghton
5	6-9	Holling	*Minn of the Mississippi*	Houghton
5	5-10	Hoppen-stedt	*The Mystery of the Deserted Village*	Watts
5	4-8	Horn	*The New Home*	Scribner
5	4-8	Huber	*They Were Brave and Bold*	Harper
5	6-10	Humphre-ville	*The Years Between*	Scott, Foresman

5	6-12	Hyde	*Atoms Today and Tomorrow*	McGraw
5	4-8	Hyde	*Off Into Space!*	McGraw
5-6	4-12	Irving	*Volcanoes and Earthquakes*	Knopf
5	5-9	Jackson	*Bud Plays Junior High Basketball*	Hastings
5	6-9	Jagendorf	*The Gypsies' Fiddle and Other Gypsy Tales*	Vanguard
5	5-8	Johnson	*Rolf, and Elkhound of Norway*	Harcourt
5	5-10	Johnsen	*Enchanted Isles*	Merrill
5	3-9	Kettelkamp	*The Magic of Sound*	Morrow
5	6-9	Kipling	*The Jungle Book*	Doubleday
5	4-12	Kohn	*Our Tiny Servants: Molds and Yeasts*	Prentice
5	5-12	Kohn	*The Peaceful Atom*	Prentice
5	5-9	Lattimore	*The Bittern's Nest*	Morrow
5	3-8	Lattimore	*Peachblossom*	Harcourt
5	4-12	Lauber	*Big Dreams and Small Rockets*	Crowell
5	6-9	Lawson	*Ben and Me*	Little
5	6-9	Lawson	*Mr. Revere and I*	Little
5	6-9	Lawson	*The Great Wheel*	Viking
5	6-9	Lawson	*They Were Strong and Good*	Viking
5	4-8	Leaf	*History Can Be Fun*	Lippincott
5	2-8	Leaf	*Manners Can Be Fun*	Lippincott
5	3-8	Leaf	*Safety Can Be Fun*	Lippincott
5	5-8	Lenski	*Prairie School*	Lippincott
5	5-8	Lenski	*Strawberry Girl*	Lippincott
5	6-12	Lent	*Flight Overseas*	Macmillan
5	6-9	Lewellen	*The Boy Scientist: A Popular Mechanics Book*	Golden
5-6	5-10	Lewellen	*You and Transportation*	Childrens
5	5-8	Lofting	*Dr. Dolittle's Circus*	Lippincott
5	5-8	Lofting	*Story of Dr. Dolittle*	Lippincott
5	5-12	Lord	*Peary to the Pole*	Harper
5	6-9	McCloskey	*Home Price: Centerberg Tales*	Viking
5	4-8	McClung	*Buzztail, The Story of a Rattlesnake*	Morrow
5	4-12	Malcolmson	*Yankee Doodle's Cousins*	Houghton
5-6	5-12	Malkus	*Story of Winston Churchill*	Grossett
5	4-8	Mason	*Smiling Hill Farm*	Ginn
5	4-9	Meadow-croft	*Holding the Fort with Daniel Boone*	Crowell
5-6	5-12	Meadow-croft	*Land of the Free*	Crowell
5-6	5-10	Meadow-croft	*Scarab for Luck*	Crowell
5	6-12	Miers	*The Rainbow Book of American History*	World
5	6-9	Mirsky	*Thirty-one Brothers and Sisters*	Follett
5	6-12	Moderow, et al.	*Eight Treasured Stories*	Scott, Foresman
5	6-12	Moderow	*Twenty Thousand Leagues Under the Sea*	Scott, Foresman
5	6-9	Molloy	*Shooting Star Farm*	Houghton

5	5-8	Morgan	*Aquarium Book for Boys and Girls*	Scribner
5	6-9	Orton	*The Secret of the Rosewood Box*	Lippincott
5	6-9	Pace	*Old Bones, the Wonder Horse*	McGraw
5	6-12	Peare	*Jules Verne: His Life*	Holt
5	4-8	Politi	*Juanita*	Scribner
5	5-9	Poole	*Danger! Icebergs Ahead!*	Random
5	5-10	Price	*The Phantom Reindeer*	Coward
5	6-9	Reynolds	*Custer's Last Stand*	Random
5	6-9	Rifkin	*When I Grow Up I'll Be a Farmer*	Hale
5	6-9	Ripper	*Bats*	Morrow
5	6-9	Robertson	*The Crow and the Castle*	Viking
5-6	5-12	Robinson	*Breakthrough to the Big League*	Harper
5	6-7	Rounds	*Rodeo*	Holiday
5	6-9	Rounds	*Stolen Pony*	Hale
5	6-9	Rowe	*Freckled and Fourteen*	Morrow
5	6-12	Sandrus	*Famous Mysteries*	Scott, Foresman
5	6-12	Schealer	*This Way to the Stars*	Dutton
5	6-12	Scheib	*What Happened? The Science Stories Behind the News*	McKay
5	5-10	Schiller	*The Kitchen Knight*	Holt
5	5-12	Schneider	*Everyday Weather and How It Works*	McGraw
5	5-8	Schneider	*Let's Look Inside Your House*	Scott, W. R.
5	5-8	Schneider	*Now Try This*	Hale
5	6-12	Schneider	*Wings in Your Future*	Harcourt
5	6-12	Schneider	*Everyday Machines and How They Work*	McGraw
5	4-8	Sellew	*Adventures with the Giants*	Little
5	4-8	Sellew	*Adventures with the Gods*	Little
5	4-12	Selsam	*The Language of Animals*	Morrow
5	4-8	Selsam	*Play with Plants*	Morrow
5	4-8	Selsam	*Play with Trees*	Morrow
5	6-9	Seredy	*The Good Master*	Viking
5	6-9	Seredy	*Plilomena*	Viking
5	5-8	Sharp	*Chichi's Magic*	Steck
5	5-12	Snow	*Henry Hudson: Explorer of the North*	Houghton
5	5-12	Sobol	*Encyclopedia Brown*	Nelson
5	6-9	Sootin	*Let's Go to an Airport*	Putnam
5-6	5-12	Spencer	*The Yangtze: China's River Highway*	Garrard
5	4-8	Stall	*Chukchi, Hunter*	Morrow
5	5-9	Steele	*Flaming Arrows*	Harcourt
5	6-12	Stoddard	*The Story of Power*	Garden
5-6	5-12	Syme	*African Traveler: The Story Of Mary Kingsley*	Morrow
5-6	5-12	Syme	*Balboa, Finder of the Pacific*	Morrow
5-6	5-12	Syme	*Captain Cook, Pacific Explorer*	Morrow
5	6-9	Syme	*DeSoto, Finder of the Mississippi*	Morrow
5	6-9	Syme	*Henry Hudson*	Morrow
5	6-9	Syme	*Magellan, First Around the World*	Morrow

5	4-8	Tarry	My Dog Rinty	Viking
5	5-8	Thompson	The Blue-Stone Mystery	Abelard
5	6-9	Travers	Mary Poppins	Harcourt
5	6-9	Travers	Mary Poppins Comes Back	Harcourt
5	5-8	Tunis	Keystone Kids	Harcourt
5	4-8	Urmston	Mystery of the Old Barn	Doubleday
5	5-12	Verral	Jets	Prentice
5	5-12	Verral	Robert Goddard: Father of the Space Age	Prentice
5-6	6-9	Viereck	The Summer I Was Lost	Day
5	5-7	Webb	Aguk of Alaska	Prentice
5	4-8	Webber	Bits That Grow Big	Scott, W. R.
5	5-12	Weidling	Secret of the Old Bridge	McKay
5	5-12	Welty	Birds with Bracelets	Prentice
5	5-8	Wheeler	Joseph Haydn: The Merry Little Peasant	Dutton
5	5-8	Wheeler	Sebastian Bach: The Boy from Thuringia	Dutton
5	5-8	Wheeler	Sing for America	Dutton
5-9	5-10	Wheeler	Peter Tschaikowsky	Dutton
5	4-12	Wheeler	The Story of Birds of North America	Harvey
5	5-8	Wilder	Farmer Boy	Harper
5	5-8	Wilder	Little House on the Prairie	Harper
5	6-9	Wilder	Little House in the Big Woods	Hale
5	5-8	Williams	Danny Dunn and the Homework Machine	McGraw
5	5-8	Williams	Danny Dunn and the Weather Machine	McGraw
5	6-7	Wilson	This Boy Cody	Watts
5	6-9	Wilson	Thad Owen	Hale
5-6	5-12	Winders	Sam Colt and His Gun	Day
5	5-8	Witty	You and the Constitution of the U. S.	Childrens
5	4-9	Worcester	Lone Hunter's First Buffalo Hunt	Walck
5	6-9	Worcester	Lone Hunter's Gray Pony	Walck
5	5-12	Wormser	Ride a Northbound Horse	Morrow
5	6-9	Yates	Boy's Book of Tools	Harper
5	6-9	Zim	Alligators and Crocodiles	Morrow
5	6-9	Zim	Dinosaurs	Morrow
5	6-9	Zim	Our Senses and How They Work	Morrow
5	6-9	Zim	Rabbits	Morrow
5-6	5-12	Zim	The Universe	Morrow

Grade 6

READING LEVEL	INTEREST LEVEL	AUTHOR	TITLE	PUBLISHER
6	6-11	Crary	Pocketful of Raisins	McKay
6-7	6-12	Crouse	Alexander Hamilton and Aaron Burr	Random
6	7-9	Dale	The Secret Motorcar	Harper
6	6-12	Day	The Story of Australia	Random
6	6-12	DeJong	The House on Charlton Street	Scribner
6	7-12	DeKruif	Microbe Hunters	Harcourt

6	6-12	Digby	*Baseball for Boys*	Follett
6	7-9	DuBois	*The Twenty-one Balloons*	Viking
6	7-12	DuJardin	*Practically Seventeen*	Lippincott
6	7-9	Enright	*The Melendy Family*	Holt
6	6-12	Epstein	*The First Book of the United Nations*	Watts
6	7-9	Farley	*The Black Stallion and Satan*	Random
6	7-9	Fenner	*Horses, Horses, Horses*	Watts
6	7-12	Floherty	*Behind the Silver Shield (revised)*	Lippincott
6	6-12	Fox	*Ambush at Fort Dearborn*	Martins
6	6-12	Fuller	*The Jade Jaguar Mystery*	Abingdon
6-7	6-11	Heuman	*City High Five*	Dodd
6	5-12	Hughes	*The First Book of Africa*	Watts
6	7-9	Hunt	*Better Known as Johnny Appleseed*	Lippincott
6	7-9	Hyde	*Where Speed is King*	McGraw
6	7-9	James	*Smoky, the Cowhorse*	Scribner
6	7-9	Judson	*Bruce Carries the Flag*	Follett
6	7-12	Judson	*The Green Ginger Jar*	Houghton
6	7-9	Keating	*Kid Brother*	Westminister
6	7-12	Kjelgaard	*Wildlife Cameraman*	Holiday
6	7-9	Knight	*Lassie Come Home*	Grosset
6	7-12	Lawson	*Strange Sea Stories*	Viking
6	6-12	Lobsenz	*The First Book of National Parks*	Watts
6	7-12	London	*Call of the Wild*	Macmillan
6	6-12	McNeer	*The Alaska Goldrush*	Random
6	7-9	McNeer	*Armed with Courage*	Abingdon
6	7-12	Manton	*The Story of Albert Schweitzer*	Abelard
6	7-12	Marshall	*Julie's Heritage*	McKay
6	6-12	Montgomery	*Crazy Kill Range*	World
6-7	6-12	Morris	*The First Book of the American Revolution*	Watts
6	7-9	O'Brien	*Silver Chief, Dog of the North*	Holt
6	6-12	Offit	*Cadet Quarterback*	St. Martins
6-7	6-12	Papashvily	*Louisa May Alcott*	Houghton
6	7-9	Pyle	*Some Merry Adventures of Robin Hood*	Scribner
6-7	6-12	Robinson	*Stan Musial: Baseball's Durable Man*	Putnam
6	7-9	Schoor	*Joe Di Maggio: The Yankee Clipper*	Messner
6	7-9	Selsam	*See Through the Jungle*	Harper
6	7-9	Shaffer	*The Crocodile Tomb*	Holt
6	7-12	Shapiro	*The Sal Maglie Story*	Messner
6	7-9	Syme	*Balboa: Finder of the Pacific*	Morrow
6-7	6-12	Syme	*Nigerian Pioneer: The Story of Mary Slessor*	Morrow
6	7-12	Tallant	*Evangeline and the Acadians*	Random
6	5-10	Taylor	*Jim Long-Knife*	Whitman, Albert
6	7-12	Terhune	*Lad: A Dog*	Dutton
6	7-12	Tunis	*Schoolboy Johnson*	Morrow

6	7-12	Tunis	*Buddy and the Old Pro*	Morrow
6	7-12	Tunis	*All-American*	Harcourt
6	6-12	Webb	*The Living J.F.K.*	Grosset
6	7-12	Whittam	*The Whale Hunters*	World
6	7-12	Wiggin	*Rebecca of Sunnybrook Farm*	Houghton
6	6-12	Wooley	*Libby Looks for a Spy*	Morrow
6	6-10	Wooley	*Look Alive, Libby!*	Morrow
6	7-9	Wyss	*Swiss Family Robinson*	Grosset
6	7-12	Zarchy	*Stamp Collector's Guide*	Knopf
6	**6-9**	Albrecht	*The Grist Mill Secret*	Hastings
6	7-12	Alcott	*Little Women: or Meg, Jo Beth and Amy*	Little
6	7-12	Anderson	*Touch of Greatness*	Macmillan
6	7-12	Archibald	*Full Count*	Macrae
6	7-9	Beals	*The Rush for Gold*	Harper
6	6-10	Beatty	*Bonanza Girl*	Morrow
6	7-9	Beery	*Young Teens Talk It Over*	McGraw
6	7-9	Bendick	*Electronics for Young People*	McGraw
6	7-12	Betz	*Your Manners Are Showing*	Grosset
6	7-9	Blair	*Davy Crockett: Frontier Hero*	Coward
6	7-9	Boylston	*Sue Barton, Student Nurse*	Little
6	7-9	Brill	*Madeleine Takes Command*	McGraw
6	7-9	Brink	*Magical Melons*	Macmillan
6	7-9	Brown	*John Paul Jones*	Harper
6	6-12	Buehr	*The First Book of Machines*	Watts
6	7-9	Burack, (Ed.)	*Four-Star Plays for Boys*	Plays
6-7	6-12	Carson	*Hotshot: A Basketball Story*	Farrar
6	7-9	Clemens	*Adventures of Tom Sawyer*	Grosset
6-7	6-12	Coatsworth	*Jock's Island*	Viking
6-7	6-12	Coggins	*Flashes and Flags: The Story of Signaling*	Dodd
6	7-9	Colby	*Six Shooter: Pistols, Revolver and Automatics Past and Present*	Coward
6	7-12	Coolidge	*Greek Myths*	Houghton
6	7-12	Coombs	*Rockets, Missiles and Moons*	Morrow

Grade 7

READING LEVEL	INTEREST LEVEL	AUTHOR	TITLE	PUBLISHER
7	6-12	Bee	*Make the Team in Basketball*	Grosset
7	7-12	Bishop	*Lonesome End*	Lippincott
7	7-12	Blassingame	*The U.S. Frogmen of World War II*	Random
7	7-12	Blue	*The Mouse-Gray Stallion*	Bobbs
7	7-12	Burt	*Wind Before the Dawn*	Day
7	7-12	Clewes	*Guide Dog*	Coward
7	6-12	Decker	*Long Ball to Left Field*	Morrow
7	7-12	DeGering	*Seeing Fingers: The Story of Louis Braille*	McKay
7	7-12	Farley	*The Black Stallion and Flame*	Random
7	7-12	Gault	*Drag Strip*	Dutton

7	7-12	Herron	*Dynamite Johnny O'Brien Alaska's Sea Captain*	Messner
7	6-12	Jackson	*Freshman Forward*	McGraw
7	7-12	Moody	*Wells Fargo*	Houghton
7	6-12	Peare	*Jules Verne: His Life*	Holt
7	7-12	Weaver	*Making Our Government Work: The Challenge of American Citizenship*	Coward
7	7-12	Wells	*Five-Yard Fuller*	Putnam
7	7-12	Whittlesey	*U.S. Peace Corps*	Coward
7	6-12	Yates	*Amos Fortune: Free Man*	Dutton

Grade 8

READING LEVEL	INTEREST LEVEL	AUTHOR	TITLE	PUBLISHER
8	8-12	Austen	*Pride and Prejudice*	Globe
8	8-12	Bailey and Leavell	*Worlds of People*	American
8	8-12	Benary-Isbert	*Rowan Farm*	Harcourt
8	8-12	Benary-Isbert	*The Ark*	Winston
8	8-12	Brewton, et al.	*New Horizons through Reading and Literature, Book 2*	Laidlaw
8	8-12	Daly	*Seventeenth Summer*	Dodd
8	8-12	Dickens	*A Tale of Two Cities*	Laidlaw
8	8-12	Dumas	*The Count of Monte Cristo*	Globe
8	8-12	Eliot	*Silas Marner*	Globe
8	8-12	Eliot	*The Mill on the Floss*	Globe
8	8-12	Emery	*Senior Year*	Westminster
8	8-12	Forbes	*Johnny Tremain*	Houghton
8	8-12	Forester	*The African Queen*	Modern
8	8-12	Frank	*Diary of Anne Frank*	Doubleday
8	8-12	Godden	*Episode of Sparrows*	Viking
8	8-12	Harkins	*Son of the Coach*	Holiday
8	8-12	Harkins	*Young Skin Diver*	Morrow
8	8-12	Hawthorne	*The Scarlet Letter*	Globe
8	8-12	Hersey	*Hiroshima*	Knopf
8	8-12	Hilton	*Lost Horizon*	Grosset
8	8-12	Hilton	*Random Harvest*	Little
8	8-12	Hunt	*Conquest of Everett*	Grosset
8	8-12	Lederer and Burdick	*The Ugly American*	Norton
8	8-12	London	*White Fang*	Grosset
8	8-12	Lord	*A Night to Remember*	Holt
8	8-12	Lovrein, et al.	*Adventures for Today*	Harcourt
8	8-12	MacLean	*Guns of Navarone*	Doubleday
8	8-12	Meader	*T Model Tommy*	Harcourt
8	8-12	Michener	*The Bridges at Toko-Ri*	Random
8	8-12	Montgomery	*Anne of Green Gables*	Grosset

8	8-12	Moore	*The Baby Sitter's Guide*	Crowell
8	8-12	Remarque	*All Quiet on the Western Front*	Little
8	8-12	Russel and Gunn	*Windows on the World*	Ginn
8	8-12	Salinger	*Catcher in the Rye*	Grosset
8	8-12	Smith	*A Tree Grows in Brooklyn*	Harper
8	8-12	Spencer, *et al.*	*Progress on Reading Roads*	Lyons
8	8-12	Steinbeck	*Of Mice and Men*	Bantam
8	8-12	Steinbeck	*The Pearl*	Viking
8	8-12	Steinbeck	*The Short Reign of Peppin IV*	Viking
8	8-12	Twain	*Connecticut Yankee*	Globe
8	8-12	Verne	*Twenty Thousand Leagues Under the Sea*	Scribner
8	8-12	Wells	*War of the Worlds*	Harper

CHAPTER 8

Organization, Implementation, and Administration of Programs for Individuals With Reading Difficulties

T HIS CHAPTER ON administration is included in a book concerned with *teaching* because the teacher should be the central
figure in the organization, implementation, and administration
of the special reading program. Historically, there has been
difficulty in getting English and American educators to recognize the importance of the teacher's role in administration. Part
of this problem has been due to teachers' poor self-concepts.
There seems to be an idea that teachers' complete subservience
to administrators is part of being "dedicated" and "professional."
Unless teachers and administrators can work together in an atmosphere of mutual respect, it is the students and the program
that will suffer.

SELECTION OF THE TEACHER

Much conflict can be avoided if the administrators selecting
the teacher will openly and honestly answer the following question: Do we want a teacher who will run this program, or a
teacher who can be run by the administration? The answer will
depend, to some extent, upon how secure the administration is.

To fill a position of this type, the teacher should have a
strong personality, be only moderately flexible, have a sense of
humor, be compassionate toward students rather than overly
sympathetic, and be dedicated to teaching rather than to professional recognition. The teacher should have academic spe-
cializations in both reading and learning difficulties and should
have considerable training in child development and psychology.

A high grade point average in college work is not necessarily a recommendation for this type of position because teachers who themselves had had some trouble in school often make the best teachers of students with learning difficulties. Other things being equal, it may be found that a man fills this position better than a woman, and that a married woman with children fills it better than a single woman. Sometimes younger teachers will be found to have more stamina and better nerves than older ones, but older teachers often have more patience. Teaching other types of special classes and proficiency in teaching lower grade reading may tend to provide the teacher of individuals with learning difficulties with a good experimental background.

SELECTION OF THE ORGANIZATIONAL PLAN

The type of organizational plan selected depends upon a number of factors:
1. The nature of the learning problems involved.
2. The wishes of the teacher selected to run the program.
3. The amount of money available.
4. The facilities available.
5. The attitudes of other staff members toward the program.

Self-Contained Special Classroom

The self-contained classroom is one of the more traditional organizational patterns that we have inherited from special education. A small group of students spends all or most of its day with the special teacher. The self-contained classroom organization does not necessarily mean that the students do not leave the classroom for some subjects or that these subjects cannot be taught by other teachers. Desirable features of the self-contained classroom include the emotional support which can be given the students throughout the day by the special teacher, the teacher's extensive knowledge of the students by having them all day, and the continuity of a program in which reading skills can be emphasized throughout the school day. Drawbacks to this kind of organizational plan include the possibility that the group will become too ingrown—that the students may fail to achieve sufficient social independence, the calling of attention to the ways these youngsters differ from other students because of their being segregated for most of the school day, and the need of the reading teacher to devote much of his time to instruction in non-reading skills.

Special Homeroom

In the special homeroom, the students receive most of their reading and language arts work from the specialist, but may go to other classrooms for a major part of their school day. This plan has many of the advantages of the self-contained classroom, plus the fact that the students have opportunities for wider association with their nonhandicapped peers. Factors operating against this type of plan are that other teachers may feel that the specialist is not earning his pay when he does not have a full classroom and that he is "dumping" his students on other teachers.

Clinic or Learning Laboratory

This organizational pattern is based upon the older conception of the reading laboratory. The students spend most of their time in a regular classroom and come to the clinic individually or in small groups for special reading and/or language arts instruction. Advantages of this plan are that all the teacher's time can be given to reading instruction, groups can be based upon instructional needs, and regular classroom instructors often perceive this plan as a means of taking problem children off their hands. Disadvantages of the clinic or learning laboratory are that little continuity of reading instruction takes place during the remainder of the day and little opportunity is provided for the special teacher to give the students continuing emotional support.

Teacher-Consultant in a Resource Room

In this type of set-up, the teacher spends part of his time working with individuals who have reading difficulties and the remainder of his time as a resource person providing special services to teachers in regular classrooms. These services include testing students, teaching classroom teachers specialized techniques, and providing regular teachers with special materials. This plan is based upon the philosophy that every youngster should eventually be taken care of in his own classroom and that every teacher should become able to effectively instruct children with learning difficulties. At this time, the practicality of implementing this philosophy remains to be proven. The teacher-consultant plan has most of the advantages of the clinic or learning laboratory as well as the advantage of helping the classroom teacher fulfill his responsibility toward the child with a reading difficulty. One disadvantage is that the classroom teacher may lack the time or desire to carry through on the recommendations of the specialist.

INTERPERSONAL RELATIONSHIPS

Good interpersonal relationships actually form the basis for the smooth operation of the reading program as a whole. The program is usually as effective as the degree of cooperation attained among the personalities involved.

Students

The relationship between a remedial teacher and his students is usually a little closer than is common in the regular classroom situation. This does not mean that a familiarity that detracts from good discipline is called for. In fact, the remedial situation usually calls for more discipline and guidance than is necessary in the regular classroom situation. Our youngsters many times do not have too good a control of themselves, and often need a firm hand to give them the feeling of security and well-being that they need.

But the student often has a need to know a little about the remedial teacher as a person. Also, the student needs to feel that the teacher is interested in him as a person and not just a "case." A few minutes of informal conversation at the beginning of each period is not wasted time. On the other hand, the remedial teacher should not become a "counselor" who is there to solve all the youngster's problems for him. Sometimes the relationship between a remedial teacher and his student deteriorates into such a mutual dependency relationship that it is harmful to both.

One of the most important tasks of the special reading teacher is to attempt to improve the student's attitude toward reading. The teacher will sometimes have to support a student as he faces the reality of his learning problems. It is very important to develop in the student a commitment to learning, to replace the avoidance of success which characterizes so many of our youngsters.

Although the teacher should stay out of the student's home life as much as possible, there are times when it is necessary for the teacher to referee a child-parent conflict growing out of the youngster's learning problem. The teacher may also be called upon to help a student cope with guilt feelings connected with his learning problems.

There seems to be a current trend, even at the college and graduate school level, for the "students" to tell the teachers not only what to teach, but how to teach it. This state of affairs usually results from a combination of poor administration and weak teachers. The outcome is that there is very little structure or security present in the school. Such a situation is even more harmful to an individual with learning difficulties than to most students.

The special teacher sometimes has to deal with overt or passive hostility on the part of the students. How this hostility is handled depends upon the personalities of everyone involved. While the "soft-sell" works in some cases, a show of strength is called for at other times.

The teacher of students with learning difficulties should be careful that evaluation of student work be done in such a way that the student will not be humiliated or embarrassed. Many of these youngsters have been subjected to years of this type of harassment, and have developed some negative attitudes toward teachers. The special reading program will not usually be successful if the students feel that this performance is to be repeated.

Secretaries

As Napoleon recognized that an army travels on its stomach, so experienced teachers have come to realize that a school often travels on the efforts of its secretaries and custodians. The secretaries form a sort of "diplomatic core" which can advise a new teacher on how to get along with almost everyone in the school. If the secretaries like the teacher, they can get work done for him with a minimum of red tape. Often, a secretary can get a teacher through an emergency with a minimum of fuss and bother. Most secretaries respond to courtesy and consideration shown by a teacher.

Custodians

Custodians are in a unique position to be familiar with the various personalities in the school. The custodians can usually guide the new teacher around personality conflicts in progress. Custodians often seem to know where misplaced equipment can be found, and in a real pinch, can "borrow" things that the teacher desperately needs. Custodians are sometimes more sympathetic toward students with learning problems than are other teachers. Custodians will tend to be more friendly toward the special program if the teacher sees to it that the students are well behaved and not destructive.

Other Teachers

It is important that the special teacher maintain good relations with regular classroom teachers, not only for his own peace of mind, but also for the welfare of his students. If students are to be shared with regular classroom teachers for part of the day, it is especially important that all the teachers involved be able to cooperate. The special teacher needs the help of regular classroom teachers in coordinating his program with the general curriculum of the school district.

The special teacher can expect cooperation from classroom teachers who are secure, satisfied, and interested in students with learning problems. Conversely, the special teacher can often expect trouble from teachers who are insecure, dissatisfied, who see no need or value in working with students with learning problems, and who are the school's chronic complainers—with or without a reason.

One of the problems encountered by the special teacher is how much and what kind of help to give the regular classroom teacher when she asks about students in the regular classroom who may be having learning problems. The special teacher should be careful about giving off-the-cuff or "long distance" diagnosis. He should also beware of giving advice which may result in stepping on other specialists' toes or getting the administrator in over his head. But when advice that has been given leads to success, this does result in good relations with other teachers.

Another problem with which the special teacher may have to cope is that of cruelty on the part of some teachers toward students with learning problems. It is not uncommon for a school to have one or two teachers who will abuse the child who is different when they have contact with him in the lunch room, the hall and the playground. If the student leaves the regular classroom for specialized reading instruction, he may return to find that he will be penalized for work he missed during the period of time he was absent. If the student is assigned to the special room but comes to the regular classroom for part of his day, he may find that he is either ignored or put on the spot by the classroom teacher. This statement is not to imply that most classroom teachers have negative attitudes toward students with learning problems, but the specialist should be aware that such attitudes do exist.

Some tips on getting along with other teachers:
1. Make sure that the youngsters are especially well behaved and well disciplined outside the special classroom as well as in it.
2. Take the initiative in establishing lines of communication with other teachers.
3. Ask advice of other teachers, whether you use it or not.
4. Help other teachers obtain information that they are seeking concerning learning difficulties.
5. Stay out of the teachers' lounge until you know whether

it is a "social oasis" or a "den of iniquity" where "professionals" brew most of the mischief that goes on in the school.

Parents

It is essential that the teacher be able to communicate effectively with the parents of children who have learning difficulties. To be truly effective, this communication should be based upon an understanding of parental personalities, the socio-economic levels represented in the school, and the pressure groups operating within the school system.

Essentially, there are three types of parents of these youngsters:

1. *The Overly Helpful.* This parent is verbal. She is always on the scene, either physically, through notes, or by telephone. If a woman, she is "sweet," and if a man, he is your "buddy." Insincerity is the password of this parent, who will say one thing to your face, another to the parent who did not come to school, and something entirely different to the child when he gets home. Little carry through can be expected of this parent.

2. *The Genuinely Helpful.* This parent may not come to school on his own too often, but this is no indication that there is a lack of interest. The parent is often concerned, but not willing to place too much pressure on the child. The genuinely helpful are willing to aid both student and teacher if told exactly what to do and how to proceed.

3. *The Antagonistic.* The *openly antagonistic* is the easier of the two types of antagonistic parents to handle because this parent does want to communicate with the teacher. There may be past reasons for this parent's antagonism. Some of these may be failure of the school to communicate properly and promptly, failure of the school to do anything for the child, or a sadistic attitude on the part of a previous teacher toward the child.

    The *passively antagonistic* parent is very difficult to handle. He may listen without comment, and then do absolutely nothing to cooperate with the teacher.

Three socioeconomic levels may exhibit different attitudes toward goals of reading instruction:

1. *Lower and Lower-Middle Classes.* This group is primarily interested in how learning to read will help the student earn a living. This is a goal that the teacher can make use of if he is practical. By all means, get off the culture, Shakespeare-oriented routine.

2. *Upper-Middle and Lower-Upper Classes.* In some school systems, this group is made up, to a large extent, of the "strainers and strivers" who take their children's school careers most seriously at the neighborhood coffee klatch. The mothers of these children are often interested in the "tinsel and tinkle" of the reading curriculum, such as programs in which the children perform, busy-work projects, newspaper articles, etc. Give some of this to them and keep "city hall" happy.

3. *Upper-Upper Class.* This group is interested in reading success for use in college, business, and cultural activities. This is where a strong literary program has its place.

Formal parent conferences set up on a regular once or twice a year basis are often a waste of time. Conferences should be held when the need arises. When a conference is held, keep it moving. Be realistic. Do not make unwarranted promises. Listen. If possible, talk with the father, too.

Dealing with the P.T.A. can provide an opportunity for explaining the program to a large number of parents. If the specialist wishes to have a good attendance at his meeting, be sure to include as many students as possible in some type of program. The P.T.A. can be used to raise extra money for the reading program. At the P.T.A. meeting, the specialist should be careful not to get cornered and monopolized by one or two parents.

Sometimes parents are interested in reading about developments in reading instruction. Robinson and Rauch (1965, pp. 103-105) have presented an excellent reading list for parents.

Other Specialists

Psychologist

The psychologist is a helper and auxiliary to the teacher.

The teacher should keep in mind that the psychologist is concerned with the intellectual functioning and emotional status of the student, and is not usually an educator. The teacher should carefully outline what information he wishes from the psychologist before he examines the student. The teacher should evaluate the psychological report and request more information if the report is not found to be usable.

Speech Specialist

The speech specialist (or preferably, *language specialist*) can be one of the most helpful people to the reading specialist. The language specialist can help the reading teacher understand the relationship of a speech and/or language problem to the development of phonic skills and reading comprehension. When both the language specialist and the reading teacher are working with the same student, they should confer often so that they may reinforce each other's efforts.

School Nurse

The school nurse can do vision and hearing screening and keep health records. She can also arrange for complete physical and neurological examinations when indicated.

Social Worker and Psychiatrist

Some school systems make use of a social worker and/or a psychiatrist in connection with teaching reading to individuals with reading difficulties.

Board of Education

If the special reading program is to continue its development, it is necessary that the program have the support of the board of education. Most boards are usually composed of lay people. Board members may not favor a special program because of its cost, but may be interested in developing such a program if a "competing district" has one, or if a board member has or knows a child with a learning difficulty.

The special teacher should keep the administrator and the board informed about the progress and needs of the program. The specialist should be in attendance at board meetings at which the program is to be discussed. At times, the teacher should request permission to make reports directly to the board.

Teachers should not be afraid to do a little politicking with board members. If there is only one woman on the board, she may well be the "whip" and therefore the most important member. Parents should be encouraged to let board members know about the value of the reading program.

Administration

The teacher in the special reading program should be responsible to only one administrator. When the specialist is responsible to the building principal, the director of special education, and perhaps the superintendent as well, chaos is often the result. As far as possible, responsibility and authority for operation of the reading program should be delegated to the specialist in charge of instruction. Special administrative committees are often of very limited usefulness. The administrative personnel are responsible for supplying space, equipment, and materials as needed by the teacher.

IMPLEMENTATION OF THE READING PROGRAM

In starting the special reading program, it is better to move slowly and develop it gradually than to make a great impression at the start and then have a program which does not live up to its initial promise.

Selection of Students

Students should be chosen who have at least average intelligence as determined by an individual psychological examination administered by a qualified psychological examiner. The number of students selected for the program will depend upon such factors as the type of organizational pattern selected, the severity of the learning problems involved, and the skill and training of the teacher. In general, the teacher should start with a small number of students, and as these become familiar with the program, more can be added gradually.

It has been traditional in the field of remedial reading that pupils be selected at the beginning or end of grade three, when they are about two years retarded in reading. Actually, this is a wasteful practice. Children having trouble with reading should receive special help as early as grade one.

When starting a new program, it is standard operating procedure to select good looking, "nice" youngsters who have a good chance of succeeding. In this way, the program "sells" and early results can be shown. The special reading teacher should have the final say as to who is admitted, how many individuals are admitted, and how long they remain.

Selection of Instructional Approaches and Materials

In setting up a new program, the teacher should delay the selection of at least half of his instructional materials until after he knows what types of learning problems he will be working with. At least one quarter of the instructional budget should be reserved for emergencies which will occur during the school year. Financial provision should also be made for the reproduction of teacher-made materials. A wide variety of methods and materials must be available in order that students may be shifted from one approach to another whenever necessary. A variety of workbooks should be purchased so that these may be disassembled and pages filed according to different word attack skills and types of reading comprehension.

Operational Guidelines

Operational guidelines will vary in detail according to the type of organizational plan that has been chosen. The guidelines provided here are general enough to apply to most programs.

Getting Started

By the time a remedial plan is to be formulated, the youngster should know quite a bit about himself and his problem.

Also, the teacher should have in mind some of the techniques and materials that he is going to use.

The plan should begin with a scheme for building the youngster up so that he will get maximum benefit from remedial instruction. To plunge a student into a type of remedial instruction for which he is not ready is quite damaging to the student's concept of himself as a learner. Remedial instruction is his last chance, and it should not be undertaken haphazardly.

If the student has a psychophysiological problem, this is a good place to begin the build-up. It is a basic phase of instruction, and is not so closely related to reading as to be threatening to the individual. Also, this type of treatment is something at which most people can succeed.

The next step is perceptual training, if this is indicated. It is a logical second phase of instruction because the perceptual processes develop out of the more basic psychophysiological skills. The extent to which a person can be retrained depends to a large degree upon the student's sensory endowment, his intelligence, and the willingness with which he enters into the treatment.

The needed basic reading skills can be worked on next. This is where the student is likely to balk. It is on these basic reading skills that he has failed before. Success at this stage is quite important. The teacher has to be firm if the student wants to give up. But as success begins to come, motivation becomes easier.

Instruction moves into reading easy books while the reader is still working on the basic skills. Make sure that the first selections are easy enough to give a feeling of success. (This may be a place for comic books.) The first reading is done primarily to get the student moving smoothly into the reading act. Consequently, it is wise to permit the student to choose a *topic* in which he is interested. The actual selection of the first few books will probably have to be done by the teacher to insure the choice of the proper grade level.

As the student moves into using remedial reading books for most of his work, it should be explained to him that the reading is going to become more difficult. Tell him that this is because he is progressing in the program and that he must now be prepared for a larger number of unfamiliar words and more difficult ideas. If the youngster is properly prepared for this change, he will be better able to handle it.

Near the middle of the remedial program, the teacher should help the student transfer his newly learned skills to his school work. We would like to think that this transfer will take place automatically, but this is not true in many cases. Specialized vocabulary and concepts particular to a certain field of knowledge present problems. The remedial reading teacher is in a position to help the student get started developing better ways to attack his school assignments. But if the work is highly specialized, as in high school, the cooperation of the subject matter teachers is going to be required.

This brings up a problem which points up one of the weak spots in our approach to remedial readers. There is an old adage in education that says, "Every teacher is a teacher of reading." To date, this has only been given lip service, if it has been acknowledged at all. Subject area teachers are usually the loudest in complaining that a student cannot read. But let the remedial teacher ask for some suggestions concerning how to help the student in his content subjects, and the subject area teacher suddenly becomes "professionally deaf."

There are ten ways that subject area teachers in the junior and senior high schools can help the remedial student:

1. Let the remedial teacher explain the student's reading level and why he is having a difficult time with reading.
2. Realize that by the time the student gets into the upper grades it has taken him years to get this far behind in reading.
3. Do not expect the remedial reader to bring his reading up to grade level by the end of the present marking period.
4. Provide a variety of textbooks on the subject being studied by the class. Unless it is a very select group, it is as unreasonable to expect every student in a subject area class to read from the same book as it is to expect every youngster in a reading class to read from the same book.
5. Introduce new vocabulary when beginning a new section

of work. This will benefit all the students as well as those having reading difficulties.

6. Use lectures, demonstrations, and projects as well as reading from textbooks.

7. Do not require the remedial reader to read orally in class unless he insists. Such a requirement may not only humiliate him, but will usually annoy the other students and delay the progress of the class.

8. If only one textbook has to be used, permit the student's parents to read it to him at home.

9. If a simplified program is worked out for the student and he handles it satisfactorily, work out a method of grading which indicates that the work is satisfactory for this youngster's stage of educational development, but that it is still below grade level. This should be done for the teacher's own protection. If such an indication is not made, it is all too easy for the student or his parents to "misunderstand" and "believe" that the work in the subject area class is perfectly all right.

10. Remember that if the youngster is not kept profitably occupied with something that he is able to do, a discipline problem may develop. In such a case, it is not usually that the youngster cannot read because he is a discipline problem, but that he is a discipline problem because he cannot read.

Scheduling and Grouping

In spite of the old idea that the perfect size for a group is a group of one, this may not always be true. When a student is sensitive about his reading problem, he may sometimes be more comfortable when he is with a group of students having similar problems. The commonalty of type of problem is a better criterion for grouping than is numerical size. How often students should receive instruction, and for what length of time, will vary from student to student.

There seems to be a prevalent idea that special reading classes should be scheduled so that they do not conflict with other important parts of the students' school day. However, anyone who has had experience with scheduling can testify that each teacher looks upon his subject as most important, and each student wishes to be absent from the subject he dislikes the most. Generally, therefore, the reading teacher will have to set up his schedule so that students with similar instructional needs can be grouped together, regardless of existing class schedules. One exception should be the physical education program. Because of the importance of motor development in relation to reading performance and because many students with reading problems have a high need for physical activity, it is undesirable that these students be taken from physical education for reading instruction.

Record Keeping

Each student should have a folder in which his test scores and past work are kept. Students should have free access to this folder. Daily lesson plans will usually be found to be of little use to the special reading teacher. This seems to be true because of the rapidity with which changes have to be made from one instructional material to another. If the school administration insists upon lesson plans, routine plans can be turned into the office and these can later be ignored in the interest of flexible teaching.

Evaluation and Reporting

Evaluation should be an on-going process based upon standardized test scores and the judgment of the teacher. Evaluation reports should be regularly made available to students and parents as well as to other teaching personnel.

CHAPTER 9

Sources of Professional Information for the Teachers of Individuals with Learning Difficulties

WINEVA MONTOOTH GRZYNKOWICZ

IN THE DAILY PROCESS of helping children improve their reading performance, it is difficult for the teacher to keep up with the latest developments in this field. Once the teacher has developed a certain routine of dealing with remedial readers, he sometimes forgets that he should occasionally review some of the basic books in the field. Under the pressure of daily work, it is not uncommon for the teacher to skip local and regional meetings of professional organizations interested in reading and learning difficulties. These developments are an unfortunate, but understandable outcome of the overwork that some teachers are subjected to.

The other extreme is that of the teacher who reads every article in every journal, buys every new professional book that comes off the press, attends every meeting he can get to, and then uses his youngsters as guinea pigs for half-thought-out experiments. This situation results in a highly "experimental" and, in many cases, unorganized special program.

Most good programs are run by teachers who keep aware of the major developments in the field, but are not led into changing the structure of their program every time something new comes out. We need to have new ideas in the field and we must have flexible, varied programs. The teacher needs to be in touch with a moderate variety of ideas for specialized reading programs through reading selected journals, occasionally reviewing a few basic books in the field, and attending some significant professional meetings.

It is good for the teacher to occasionally review some basic books on teaching developmental reading. There is a tendency on the part of remedial teachers to think that we are a little more special than we really are. We are not special teachers—rather teachers of special children. Some good books on the teaching of developmental reading are included in the following.

SOME BOOKS ON DEVELOPMENTAL READING

Modern Reading Instruction (Cutts, 1964). This is a modern, up-to-date account of reading instruction. It is a must for today's reading teacher.

Improving the Teaching of Reading (Dechant, 1964). The strong educational-psychological basis of this book makes it an important contribution to the field. It directs the teacher's attention to the *reader* as well as the *reading process*.

The Teaching of Reading and Writing (Gray, 1956). Gray's international survey of methods of teaching reading and writing gives the remedial teacher several ideas on how to specialize instruction.

On Their Own in Reading (Gray, 1948). This is the classic book on teaching word attack skills. Actually, some reading people think that the 1948 edition is superior to the revision.

Effective Teaching of Reading (Harris, 1962). The appendices are valuable. There is one on resources for teachers of reading, a concise summary of phonics rules, and a list of publishers and their addresses.

Readings on Reading Instruction (Harris, 1963). This is a compilation of recent writings on a multitude of aspects of reading instruction. The volume is certainly a stimulating one, particularly the consideration of concept burden of instructional materials given by Mary C. Serra.

Principles and Practices of Teaching Reading (Heilman, 1961). As the title implies, this book contains a combination of theory and methods of application. The volume contains much in the way of results of modern research.

Developing Spelling Power (Russell, Murphy, and Durrell, 1957). This is a practical approach to the teaching of phonics in the spelling program. The approach is an excellent one.

Phonics in Listening, in Speaking, in Reading, in Writing (Scott and Thompson, 1962). A total approach to phonics in the language arts program is a refreshing one for the remedial teacher.

Toward Better Reading (Spache, 1963b). This is a modern treatment of reading instruction. The appendices include: "Selected Diagnostic Tests and Equipment," "Selected Equipment and Other Resources for Remedial Teaching," "Indexes and Lists of Audio-Visual Aids for Reading Instruction," and "Producers and Distributors of Audio-Visual Aids."

SOME BOOKS ON TEACHING REMEDIAL READING

Reading Difficulties: Their Diagnosis and Correction (Bond and Tinker, 1957). This is one of the more complete texts on remedial reading, written by two distinguished leaders in the field. Although there is a 1967 edition available, I tend to prefer the first edition.

Helping the Non-Reading Pupil in the Secondary School (Bullock, 1956). This is a book in a much neglected field of remedial reading. It presents the problem of the high school remedial reader in some detail and gives practical suggestions for helping him.

Remedial Techniques in Basic School Subjects (Fernald, 1943). Fernald's special visual-auditory-kinesthetic-tactile treatment is described in this classic book.

Teacher's Guide for Remedial Reading (Kottmeyer, 1959). Kottmeyer's book is especially useful because of the detailed sections on diagnosis.

Teaching the Retarded Reader: A Guide for Teachers, Reading Specialists and Supervisors (Cohn and Cohn, 1967). As indicated by the subtitle, the scope of this book is a wide one. The techniques, especially the administrative ones, are very practical and common-sense oriented.

Corrective and Remedial Teaching: Principles and Practices (Otto and McMenemy, 1966). The authors present a theoretical basis for their work; how to make a case study; diagnostic and corrective techniques in reading, spelling, arithmetic, handwriting, written and oral expression: ideas relative to the training and function of remedial teachers.

How to Increase Reading Ability (Harris, 1961). This text represents a comprehensive treatment of the practical aspects of reading instruction. The appendices containing a list of tests, a list of books for remedial reading, and a list of publishers and their addresses are quite helpful.

Reading Disability: Progress and Research Needs in Dyslexia (Money, 1962). This is a collection of writings by eminent modern workers in the field of severe learning difficulties.

Why Pupils Fail in Reading (Robinson, 1946). This is one of the classic investigations into the cause of reading disability. The volume still throws much light upon the etiology of reading problems.

Reading Disability: Diagnosis and Treatment (Roswell and Natchez, 1964). Roswell and Natchez have not only given a thorough treatment of reading disability in this book, but have listed many methods and materials useful to the remedial teacher in his everyday work.

SOME BOOKS ON LEARNING DIFFICULTIES

Educating Children with Learning Disabilities: Selected Readings (Frierson and Barbe, 1967). This book is a collection of recent articles on learning difficulties. The articles have been organized into four main parts, an "Introduction to Learning Disorders," "Specialized Approaches to Learning Disorders," "Diagnosing Learning Disorders," and "Teaching the Child with Learning Disorders." The glossary of learning disability terms is a valuable inclusion.

Educational Therapy in the Elementary School (Ashlock and Stephen, 1966). The practical and concise information given in this book makes it a good reference book for any educator, and particularly so for a teacher of children with a learning difficulty.

Achieving Perceptual-Motor Efficiency (Barsch, 1967). This volume sets forth a curriculum organization for children with learning difficulties which emphasizes the importance of physical movement.

Learning Disabilities, Educational Principles and Practices

(Johnson and Myklebust, 1967). The authors have given an extensive coverage of the theory and research connected with psychoneurological learning disabilities.

Educational Management of Children with Learning Disabilities: Minimal Brain Dysfunction (Edgington and Clements, 1967). The authors have compiled an extensive bibliography for an easy reference source to aid anyone interested in locating basic resource writings. The references listed are also cross indexed to cover nineteen separate subject areas.

· *The Brain-Injured Child in Home, School, and Community* (Cruickshank, 1967). This book provides the reader with a good background of information for understanding these children and their problems. Included are diagnostic procedures and practical techniques for the teacher and parent.

The Slow Learner in the Classroom (Kephart, 1960). Kephart is one of the pioneers in the field of learning difficulties. The title of the book may be somewhat misleading to the reader because by "slow learner," Kephart is referring to the child with learning difficulties, not the child with limited intellectual endowment. The book includes diagnostic and corrective procedures which can be used by the teacher in the regular classroom.

Prescriptive Teaching (Peter, 1965). In this book, the author advocates an eclectic diagnostic approach which appears to be suitable for children with a variety of learning difficulties. He shows how diagnostic findings can be translated into educational practice.

How to Increase Your Child's Intelligence (Getman, 1962). This easy to read booklet has been prepared for use primarily by parents. However, the teacher of children with learning difficulties will find chapter four to be of particular usefulness.

Helping the Brain-Injured Child (Siegel, 1962). This book is of particular merit because of the attention that is given to the need for developing mental health in the child with learning difficulties. It is of worth to both parents and teachers.

SOME ORGANIZATIONS AND JOURNALS

The International Reading Association, 6 Tyre Avenue, Newark, Delaware, 19711, is the main organization centered in this country which concerns itself entirely with reading. The IRA publishes two journals in which are reported the latest findings and ideas in the reading field. *The Reading Teacher* is the journal aimed at the elementary level. The *Journal of Reading* is for those working at the high school level. Membership in the International Reading Association can be very beneficial to the remedial reading teacher. *Elementary English,* the official publication of The National Council of Teachers of English, 508 South Sixth Street, Champaign, Illinois, provides the teacher of individuals with reading difficulties with information concerning modern trends in the communication skills.

Children's House is a magazine which has a strong, but modern day, Montessori orientation. The journal is published for the purpose of educating the young child at home and in the school. Articles are timely and the authors consist of authorities from a number of disciplines. The magazine can be obtained from Children's House, Inc., 2145 Central Parkway, Cincinnati, Ohio, 45214.

Membership in the Association for Children with Learning Disabilities, H.Q.—U.S. and Canada, 3739 South Delaware Place, Tulsa, Oklahoma, 74105, brings a newsletter of current events to the member. *Academic Therapy Quarterly* is a magazine dedicated to the study of learning disabilities and is published by The Dewitt Reading Clinic, Inc., 1543 Fifth Avenue, San Rafael, California, 94901.

For the teacher working with more severely handicapped children, membership in the Council for Exceptional Children, NEA, 1201 Sixteenth Street, N. W., Washington, D. C., 20036, is almost essential. *Exceptional Children* is the journal published by this organization.

References

ABERCROMBIE, M. L. J.; GARDINER, P. A.; HANSEN, E.; JONCKHEERE, J.; LINDON, R. L.; SOLOMON, G., and TYSON, M. C.: Visual, perceptual and visuomotor impairment in physically handicapped children. *Percept Mot Skills Monogr Suppl,* 3:18, 1964.

ABRAHAM, W.: *How to Improve Your Reading and Vocabulary Growth.* Chicago, Coronet Instructional Films, 1963.

ADAMS, FAY; GRAY, LILLIAN, and REESE, DORA: *Teaching Children to Read.* New York, Ronald, 1949.

ALLPORT, G.: *Pattern and Growth in Personality.* New York, Holt, 1961.

American Association for Health, Physical Education and Recreation: *Children and Fitness.* Washington, Amer Ass Hlth, Phys Ed Rec, 1960.

American Association for Health, Recreation and Physical Education: *Your Child Can't Sit and Keep Fit.* Washington, Amer Ass Hlth, Rec Phys Ed, 1961.

ANDREWS, GLADYS: *Creative Rhythmic Movement for Children.* Englewood Cliffs (N.J.), Prentice-Hall, 1954.

ASHLOCK, P.: *The Ashlock Inventory of Word Attack Skills.* Chicago, Ashlock Learning Center, 1968.

ASHLOCK, P.: *Visual Perception of Children in the Primary Grades and its Relation to Reading Performance.* Austin, U of Tex Library; Ann Arbor, Michigan Univ, Microfilms, 1963.

ASHLOCK, P.: *Developing Mental Health in Children with Learning Difficulties.* Chicago, Ashlock Learning Center, 1968.

ASHLOCK, P.: *The Teacher's Manual for the Ashlock Inventory of Word Attack Skills.* Chicago, Ashlock Learning Center, 1968.

ASHLOCK, P., and STEPHEN, ALBERTA: *Educational Therapy in the Elementary School.* Springfield, Thomas, 1966.

Athletic Institute: *Physical Education for Children of Elementary School Age.* Chicago, Athletic Institute, 1951.

AVERY, MARIEL and HIGGINS, ALICE: *Help Your Child Learn How to Learn.* Englewood Cliffs (N.J.), Prentice-Hall, 1962.

BAKER, H. J., and LELAND, BERNICE: *Detroit Tests of Learning Aptitude.* Cincinnati, Public School Publishing, 1958.

Bank Street College of Education: *Bank Street Readers.* New York, Macmillan, 1966.

BARSCH, R. H.: *Achieving Perceptual-Motor Efficiency: A Space Oriented Approach to Learning.* Seattle, Special Child Publications, 1967.

BARTON, A., and WILDER, D.: *Columbia-Carnegie Study of Reading Research and Its Communication.* New York, Scholastic Magazines, 1962.

BATEMAN, BARBARA: Learning disorders. *Rev Educ Res, 36:*93-119, 1966.

BEASLEY, JANE: *Slow to Talk.* New York, Teachers College Press, 1956.

BELL, R. C.: *Board and Table Games from Many Civilizations.* New York, Oxford U. P., 1960.

BELMONT, LILLIAN, and BIRCH, H. G.: Lateral dominance and right-left awareness in normal children. *Child Develop, 34:*257-270, 1963.

BENDER, L., and SILVER, A.: Body image problems of the brain-injured child. *J Soc Issues, 4:*84-89, 1948.

BENTON, A. L.: Development of finger-localization capacity in school children. *Child Develop, 26:*225-230, 1955.

BENTON, A. L.: *Right-left Discrimination and Finger Localization.* New York, Hoeber, 1959.

BENTON, A. L.; HUTCHEON, J. F., and SEYMOR, ELSIE: Arithmetic ability, finger localization capacity, and right-left discrimination in normal and defective children. *Amer J Orthopsychiat, 21:*756-766, 1951.

BENTON, A. L., and SCHULTZ, L. M.: Observations on tactual form perception (stereognosis) in preschool children. *J. Clin Psychol, 5:*359-364, 1949.

BERDARD, I.: *Gymnastics for Boys.* Chicago, Follett, 1962.

BERGER, H. J.: *Program Activities for Camps.* Minneapolis, Burgess, 1961.

BETTS, E. A.: *Foundations of Reading Instruction.* New York, American Book, 1957.

BINET, A., and SIMON, T.: *Mentally Retarded Children.* New York, Longmans, Green, 1914.

BOND, G. L., and BOND, EVA: *Teaching the Child to Read.* New York, Macmillan, 1943.

BOND, G. L.; CLYMER, T., and HOYT, C. J.: *Silent Reading Diagnostic Tests: The Developmental Reading Tests.* Chicago, Lyons & Carnahan, 1955.

BOND, G. L., and TINKER, M. A.: *Reading Difficulties: Their Diagnosis and Correction.* New York, Appleton, 1957 (Rev. 1967)

BOSTWICK, G.; BOSTWICK, G., and MIDLOCH, M.: *Lessons for Self Instruction in Basic Skills.* Del Monte Research Park, California Test Bureau, 1963.

BOWER, E.: *The Early Identification of Emotionally Handicapped Children in School.* Springfield, Thomas, 1960.

BOWER, E. M.: *The Education of Emotionally Handicapped Children.* Sacramento, California State Department of Education, 1961.

BROGAN, A., and HOTCHKISS, EMILY: *Dialog I: An Aural-Oral Course in Phonics.* Chester, Chester Electronic Laboratories, 1963.

BROWN, GRACE M., and COTTRELL, ALICE B.: *California Phonics Survey* Del Monte Research Park, California Test Bureau, 1956-1963.

BUCHANAN, CYNTHIA D., and SULLIVAN ASSOCIATES: *Programmed Reading.* St. Louis, Webster Division of McGraw-Hill, 1963-1964.

BULLOCK, H.: *Helping the Non-Reading Pupil in the Secondary School.* New York, Teachers College Press. Columbia University, 1956.

BURNS, T., and MICOLEAU, T.: *Tumbling Techniques Illustrated.* New York, Ronald, 1957.

BUROS, O. K.: *Tests in Print.* Highland Park (N.J.), Gryphon, 1961.

BUROS, O. K.: *The Sixth Mental Measurements Yearbook.* Highland Park (N.J.), Gryphon, 1965.

BUTTS, R. F., and CREMIN, L. A.: *A History of Education in American Culture.* New York, Holt, 1953.

CAMPAYRÈ, G.: *History of Pedagogy.* Boston, Heath, 1885.

CLARK, RUTH M.: Language and behavior of children with unsuspected brain injury. *Logos,* 5:26-34, 1962.

CLEMENTS, S. D. (ED.): *Minimal Brain Dysfunction in Children.* Washington, U.S. Government Printing Office, 1966.

COBB, S.: *Foundations of Neuropsychiatry.* Baltimore, Williams & Wilkins, 1958.

COHN, STELLA M., and COHN, J.: *Teaching the Retarded Reader.* New York, Odyssey, 1967.

COLEMAN, BESSIE B.; UHL, W. L., and HOSIC, J. F.: *The Pathway to Reading: Teacher's Manual for the Primer.* Morrison, Silver Burdett, 1925-1927.

Committee on Diagnostic Reading Tests: *Diagnostic Reading Tests.* Mountain Home, Committee on Diagnostic Reading Tests, 1947-1963.

Cooperative Test Division: *Sequential Tests of Educational Progress: Reading.* Princeton, Cooperative Test Division, 1963.

COWELL, C. C., and HAZELTON, HELEN: *Curriculum Designs in Physical Education.* Englewood Cliffs (N.J.), Prentice-Hall, 1955.

CRATTY, B. J.: *Developmental Sequences of Perceptual-Motor Tasks: Movement Activities for Neurologically Handicapped and Retarded Children and Youth.* Freeport, Educational Activities, 1967.

CRUICKSHANK, W. M.: *The Brain Injured Child in Home, School, and Community.* Syracuse, Syracuse University Press, 1967.

CRUICKSHANK, W. M.; BENTZEN, FRANCES A.; RATZEBURG, F. H., and TANNHAUSER, MIRIAM T.: *A Teaching Method for Brain-Injured and Hyperactive Children.* Syracuse, Syracuse University Press, 1961.

CRUICKSHANK, W. M.; BICE, H. V., and WALLEN, N. E.: *Perception and Cerebral Palsy.* Syracuse, Syracuse University Press, 1957.

CURETON, T. K.: *Physical Fitness and Dynamic Health.* New York, Dial, 1965.

CUTTS, W. G.: *Modern Reading Instruction.* New York, Center for Applied Research in Education, 1964.

DALEY, W. T. (ED.): *Speech and Language Therapy with the Brain Damaged Child.* Washington, Catholic University of American Press, 1962.

DARROW, MAY G.: *The Posture Problem Up to Date.* New York, Vantage, 1959.

DAUER, V. P.: *Fitness for Elementary School Children Through Physical Education.* Minneapolis, Burgess, 1964.

DAVIES, EVELYN A.: *The Elementary School Child and His Posture Patterns.* New York, Appleton, 1958.

DAVIS, ALLISON: *Social-Class Influences Upon Learning.* Cambridge, Harvard, 1948.

DAVIS, F. B., and DAVIS, CHARLOTTE C.: *Davis Reading Test.* New York, Psychological Corporation, 1956-1962.

DECHANT, E. V.: *Improving the Teaching of Reading.* Englewood Cliffs (N.J.), Prentice-Hall, 1964.

DE HIRSCH, KATRINA: Tests designed to discover potential reading difficulties at the six-year-old level. *Amer J Orthopsychiat, 27*:566-576, 1957.

DELACATO, C. H.: *The Diagnosis and Treatment of Speech and Reading Problems,* Springfield, Thomas, 1959.

DELACATO, C. H.: *The Treatment and Prevention of Reading Problems.* Springfield, Thomas, 1963.

DELACATO, C. H.: *Neurological Organization and Reading.* Springfield, Thomas, 1966.

DOLCH, E. W.: *Picture Word Cards.* Scarsdale, (N.Y.), Garrard, 1941.

DOLL, E. A.: The essentials of an inclusive concept of mental deficiency. *Amer J Ment Defic, 46*:214-219, 1941.

DOMAN, G. J., and DELACATO, C. H.: *Doman-Delacato Reading Program.* Chicago, Quadrangle, 1964.

DOMAN, G. J.; DELACATO, C. H., and DOMAN, R. J.: *The Doman-Delacato Developmental Mobility Scale.* Philadelphia, Rehabilitation Center, 1960.

DOMAN, G.; DELACATO, C., and DOMAN, R.: *The Doman-Delacato Developmental Language Scale.* Philadelphia, Rehabilitation Center, 1961.

EDGINGTON, RUTH, and CLEMENTS, S. D.: *Educational Management of Children with Learning Disabilities: Minimal Brain Dysfunction.* Chicago, Argus, 1967.

EDMAN, I.: *Philosopher's Quest.* New York, Viking, 1947.

Educational Developmental Laboratories: *Controlled Reader.* Huntington, Educational Developmental Laboratories, 1959-1967.

ENGLISH, H. B., and ENGLISH, AVA C.: *A Comprehensive Dictionary of Psychological and Psychoanalytical Terms.* New York, McKay, 1958.

EVANS, RUTH: *40 Basic Rhythms for Children*. New York, Putnam (U.S. Textbook), 1958.

FARNHAM, G. L.: *The Sentence-Method of Reading*. Syracuse, Bardeen, 1895.

FERNALD, GRACE M.: *Remedial Techniques in Basic School Subjects*. New York, McGraw, 1943.

FISHER, DOROTHY C.: *The Montessori Manual for Teachers and Parents*. Cambridge, Bentley, 1964.

FISHER, DOROTHY C.: *Montessori for Parents*. Cambridge, Bentley, 1965.

FREEMAN, K. J.: *Schools of Hellas*. London, Macmillan, 1908.

FREIDUS, ELIZABETH S.: New approaches in special education of the brain injured child. Reprinted by the New York Association for Brain Injured Children from *Educ Spec*, New York, Hunter College Chapter of the Council for Exceptional Children, 1957.

FRIERSON, E. C., and BARBE, W. B.: *Educating Children With Learning Difficulties*. New York, Appleton, 1967.

FROSTIG, MARIANNE: *Marianne Frostig Developmental Test of Visual Perception*. Palo Alto (Calif.), Consulting Psychologists Press, 1961.

FROSTIG, MARIANNE: In collaboration with LEFEVER, W., and WHITTLESEY, J.: *Administration and Scoring Manual for the Marianne Frostig Developmental Test of Visual Perception*. Palo Alto (Calif.), Consulting Psychologists Press, 1964.

FROSTIG, MARIANNE, and HORNE, D.: *The Frostig Program for the Development of Visual Perception*. Chicago, Follett, 1964.

FROSTIG, MARIANNE; LEFEVER, W., and WHITTLESEY, J.: A developmental test of visual perception for evaluating normal and neurologically handicapped children. *Percep Mot Skills, 12*:383-394, 1961.

FROSTIG, MARIANNE; MASLOW, P.; LEFEVER, W., and WHITTLESEY, J.: *The Marianne Frostig Developmental Test of Visual Perception: 1963 Standardization*. Palo Alto (Calif.), Consulting Psychologists Press, 1963a.

FROSTIG, MARIANNE; MASLOW, P.; LEFEVER, W., and WHITTLESEY, J.: Visual perceptual development and school adjustment and progress (abstract). *Amer J Orthopsychiat 33*:665-671, 1963b.

GANS, ROMA: *Fact and Fiction about Phonics*. Indianapolis, Bobbs, 1963.

GATES, A. I.: *The Improvement of Reading*. New York, Macmillan, 1947.

GATES, A. I., and MacGINITIE, W. H.: *Gates-MacGinitie Reading Tests*. New York, Teachers College Press, 1965 (in preparation).

GATES, A. I., and McKILLOP, ANNE S.: *Gates-McKillop Reading Diagnostic Tests*. New York, Teachers College Press, 1962.

GATES, A. I., and PEARDON, CELESTE C.: *Gates-Peardon Reading Exercises*. New York, Teachers College Press, 1963.

GELLHORN, E.: The physiology of supraspinal mechanisms. In JOHNSON, W., (ED.): *Science and Medicine of Exercise and Sports*. New York, Harper, 1960.

GESELL, A. S., and AMATRUDA, C. S.: *Developmental Diagnosis*. New York, Harper, 1947.

GETMAN, G. N.: *How to Develop Your Child's Intelligence: A Research Publication*. Luverne, Announcer, 1962.

GILMORE, J. V.: *Gilmore Oral Reading Paragraphs*. New York, Harcourt, 1951-1952.

GOOD, C. V. (ED.): *Dictionary of Education*. New York, McGraw, 1959.

GOODENOUGH, FLORENCE L., and TYLER, L. E.: *Developmental Psychology*. New York, Appleton, 1959.

GRANT, E. B., and KARLIN, R. (EDS.): *Developmental Reading*. Springfield, Illinois Curriculum Program: Office of the Superintendent of Public Instruction, 1964.

GRAY, C. T.: *Deficiencies in Reading Ability: Their Diagnosis and Treatment*. Boston, Heath, 1922.

GRAY, W. S.: *Summary of Investigations Relating to Reading. University of Chicago Supplementary Monograph, No. 28*. Chicago, U. of Chicago Press, 1925.

GRAY, W. S.: *The Teaching of Reading and Writing*. Chicago, Scott, 1956.

GRAY, W. S.: *On Their Own in Reading*. Chicago, Scott, 1948, (Rev. 1960).

HAARHOFF, T.: *Schools of Gaul*. London, Oxford, U.P., 1920.

HALSEY, ELIZABETH, and PORTER, LORENA: *Physical Education for Children, A Developmental Program*. New York, Holt (Div. of Dryden), 1958.

HARING, N. G., and PHILLIPS, E. L.: *Educating Emotionally Disturbed Children*. New York, McGraw, 1962.

HARRES, D. B.: *Childrens' Drawing as Measures of Intellectual Maturity*. New York, Harcourt, 1963.

HARRINGTON, D. A.: Communicative disorders in children. *Children*, 9:98-103, 1962.

HARRIS, A. J.: *How to Increase Reading Ability*. New York, McKay, 1961.

HARRIS, A. J.: *Effective Teaching of Reading*. New York, McKay, 1962.

HARRIS, A. J. (ED.): *Readings on Reading Instruction*. New York, McKay, 1963.

HAVIGHURST, R. J.: *Developmental Tasks and General Education*. Chicago, U. of Chicago Press, 1951.

HEALY, A., and BROMNER, AUGUSTA F.: *Delinquents and Criminals: Their Making and Unmaking*. New York, Macmillan, 1926.

HEATON, A.: *Fun Dances*. Dubuque, Brown, 1959.

HEILMAN, A. W.: *Principles and Practices of Teaching Reading*. Columbus, Merrill, 1961.

HILDRETH, GERTRUDE: *Teaching Reading*. New York, Holt, 1958.

HUEY, E. H.: *Psychology and Pedagogy of Reading*. New York, Macmillan, 1916.

HUGHES, L.: *First Book of Rhythms*. New York, Watts, 1954.

HUMPHREY, G.: *Thinking.* New York, Wiley, 1963.

JENKINS, J. J., and PATTERSON, D. G. (Eds.): *Studies in Individual Differences.* New York, Appleton, 1961.

JOHNSON, DORIS, and MYKLEBUST, H. R.: *Learning Disabilities, Educational Principles and Practices.* New York, Grune, 1967.

JOHNSON, L. B.: The President's message to congress. New York, *New York Times,* Jan. 11, 1965, p. 20.

KELLEY, ELLEN D.: *Teaching Posture and Body Mechanics.* New York, Ronald, 1949.

KEPHART, N. C.: *The Slow Learner in the Classroom.* Columbus, Merrill, 1960.

KEPHART, N. C.: *Aids to Motoric and Perceptual Training.* Bull. No. 4a, State Dep. of Pub. Instr., Madison, 16-28, 1964.

Keystone View Company: *Keystone Visual Survey Tests.* Meadville, Keystone View, 1933-1958.

KIRK, S. A.: *Teaching Reading to Slow-Learning Children.* Boston, Houghton, 1940.

KIRK, S. A.: *The Exceptional Child.* Boston, Houghton, 1962.

KIRK, S. A., and JOHNSON, G. O.: *Educating the Retarded Child.* Boston, Houghton, 1951.

KOTTMEYER, W.: *Teacher's Guide for Remedial Reading.* St. Louis, McGraw, (Webster Div.), 1959.

LARSON, L. A., and HILL, LUCILLE: *Physical Education in the Elementary School.* New York, Holt, (Dryden Div.), 1957.

Learning to Read: A Report of a Conference of Reading Experts. Princeton, Educational Testing Service, 1962.

LEAVELL, U. W., and BECK, H.: Ability of retarded readers to recognize symbols in association with lateral dominance. *Peabody J Educ,* 37:7-14, 1959.

LEWIS, R. S.; STRAUSS, A. A., and LEHTINEN, LAURA E.: *The Other Child.* New York, Grune, 1951.

LEWIS, R. S.; STRAUSS, A. A., and LEHTINEN, LAURA E.: *The Other Child.* New York, Grune, 1960.

LOWDER, R. G.: *Perceptual Forms.* Available from Winter Haven Lion's Club, Winter Haven, Florida, 1956.

LOWMAN, C., and YOUNG, C.: *Postural Fitness.* Philadelphia, Lea & F., 1960.

LUNT, LOIS: *Hop, Skip and Sing.* Minneapolis, Dennison, 1959.

LURIA, A. R.: *Role of Speech in the Regulation of Normal and Abnormal Behavior.* New York, Liveright, 1961.

LURIA, A. R. (ED.): *The Mentally Retarded Child.* New York, Macmillan, 1963a.

LURIA, A. R.: *Restoration of Function After Brain Injury.* New York, Pergamon, 1963b.

Luria, A. R.: *Higher Cortical Functions in Man*. New York, Basic Books, 1965.

Luria, A. R.: *Human Brain and Psychological Processes*. New York, Harper, 1966.

Luria, A. R., and Yudovich, F. I.: *Speech and the Development of Mental Processes in the Child*. New York, Humanities, 1959.

McCall, W. A., and Crabbs, Lelah M.: *Standard Test Lessons in Reading*. New York, Teacher College Press, 1961.

McCallister, J. M.: *Remedial and Corrective Instruction in Reading*. New York, Appleton, 1936.

McCarthy, J. J., and Kirk, S. A.: *Examiners Manual: Test of Psycholinguistic Abilities (experimental edition)*. Urbana, U. of Ill., 1961.

Magoun, M.: *The Waking Brain*. Springfield, Thomas, 1963.

Mann, H.: Method of teaching young children on their first entering school. *Common Sch J*, 6:116, 1844.

Metz, L. L.: *Action Songs and Rhythm for Children*. Minneapolis, Dennison, 1962.

Mills, R. E.: *The Teaching of Word Recognition: Including the Manual of Directions for the Learning Methods Test*. Fort Lauderdale, Mills Center, 1964.

Mirick, G. A.: *The Teaching of Reading*. Trenton, New Jersey Department of Public Instruction, 1914.

Money, J. (Ed.): *Reading Disability: Progress and Needs in Dyslexia*. Baltimore, Johns Hopkins, 1962.

Montessori, Maria: *The Discovery of Childhood*. Madras, Kalakshetra, 1948.

Montessori, Maria: *Education for a New World*. Madras, Kalakshetra, 1959.

Montessori, Maria: *The Child*. Madras, Theosophical, 1961a.

Montessori, Maria: *To Educate the Human Potential*. Madras, Kalakshetra, 1961b.

Montessori, Maria: *Reconstruction in Education*. Madras, Theosophical, 1961c.

Montessori, Maria: *The Formation of Man*. Madras, Theosophical, 1962.

Montessori, Maria: *The Absorbent Mind*. Madras, Theosophical, 1963.

Montessori, Maria: *The Montessori Method*. New York, Schocken, 1964.

Montessori, Maria: *Dr. Montessori's Own Handbook*. New York, Schocken, 1965a.

Montessori, Maria: *The Montessori Elementary Manual*. Cambridge, Bentley, 1965b.

Montessori, Maria: *Peace and Education*. Madras, Theosophical, 1965c.

Montessori, Maria: *The Secret of Childhood*. Bombay, Orient Longmans, 1965d.

Montessori, Maria: *Spontaneous Activity in Education*. New York, Schocken, 1965e.

MURRAY, RUTH L.: *Dance in Elementary Education.* New York, Harper, 1953.

NELSON, M. J.; DENNY, E. C., and BROWN, J. I.: *The Nelson-Denny Reading Test: Vocabulary-Comprehension-Rate.* Boston, Houghton, 1929-1960.

O'KEEFE, P. R., and ALDRICH, ANITA: *Education Through Physical Activities.* St. Louis, Mosby, 1959.

OLSON, W. C.: *Child Development.* Boston, Heath, 1959.

OTTO, W., and McMENEMY, R. A.: *Corrective and Remedial Teaching: Principles and Practices.* Boston, Houghton, 1966.

PANGALANGAN, VICENTA P.: *A History of Remedial Instruction in Elementary Schools in the United States.* Evanston, Northwestern University Library; Ann Arbor, Michigan, University Microfilms, 1960.

PARKER, D. H.: *S.R.A. Reading Laboratories.* Chicago, Science Research Associates, 1957-1964.

PATTERSON, S. W.: *Teaching the Child to Read.* Garden City, Doubleday, 1930.

PETER, L. J.: *Prescriptive Teaching.* New York, McGraw, 1965.

PHELPS, W. M.; KIPPHUTH, R. J. H., and GOFF, C. W.: *The Diagnosis and Treatment of Postural Defects.* Springfield, Thomas, 1956.

PHILLIPS, E. L.; WIENER, D. N., and HARING, N. G.: *Discipline, Achievement, and Mental Health.* Englewood Cliffs (N.J.), Prentice-Hall, 1960.

POLLARD, REBECCA S.: *Pollard's Synthetic Method, A Complete Manual.* Chicago, Western Publishing House, 1889.

President's Council on Youth Fitness: *Youth Physical Fitness: Suggested Elements of a School-Centered Program.* Washington, U.S. Government Printing Office, 1961.

RADLER, D. H., and KEPHART, N. C.: *Success Through Play.* New York, Harper, 1960.

RAMBUSH, NANCY M.: *Learning How to Learn.* New York, Taplinger, 1962.

Readers Digest Services: *Readers Digest Skill Builders.* Pleasantville, Readers Digest Services, 1958-1966.

ROACH, E. G., and KEPHART, N. C.: *The Purdue Perceptual-Motor Survey.* Columbus, Merrill, 1966.

ROBINSON, HELEN: *Why Pupils Fail in Reading.* Chicago, U. of Chicago Press, 1946.

ROBINSON, HELEN M., and GRAY, W. S.: *Gray Oral Reading Test.* Indianapolis, Bobbs, 1963.

ROBINSON, HELEN; MONROE, MARION; ARTLEY, A. S.; HUCH, C.; AARON, I.; WEINTRAUB, S., and GREET, W. C.: New Basic Readers (Curriculum Foundation Series, Multi-Ethnic Edition) Glenview, Scott, 1965.

ROBINSON, H. A., and RAUCH, S. J.: *Guiding the Reading Program: A Reading Consultant's Handbook.* Chicago, Science Research Associates, 1965.

ROSWELL, FLORENCE G., and CHALL, JEANNE S.: *Roswell-Chall Diagnostic Reading Test of Word Analysis Skills.* New York, Essay Press, 1956-1959.

ROSWELL, FLORENCE G., and CHALL, JEANNE S.: *Roswell-Chall Auditory Blending Test.* New York, Essay Press, 1963.

ROSWELL, FLORENCE, and NATCHEZ, GLADYS: *Reading Disability: Diagnosis and Treatment,* New York, Basic Books, 1964.

Royal Canadian Air Force: *Revised U.S. Edition of the Official Royal Canadian Air Force Exercise Plans for Physical Fitness.* New York, Pocket Bks, 1962.

RUSSELL, D. H.: *Children Learn to Read.* Boston, Ginn, 1949.

RUSSELL, KARLENE V.; MURPHY, HELEN A., and DURRELL, D. D.: *Developing Spelling Power.* New York, Harcourt, 1957.

SARASON, S.: *Psychological Problems in Mental Deficiency.* New York, Harper, 1959.

SCHAFF, P. and WACE, H.: *Select Library of Nicene and Post-Nicene Fathers of the Christian Church; (second series), vol. 6.* New York, The Christian Literature Company, 1893.

SCHILDER, P.: *The Image and Appearance of the Human Body.* New York, Wiley, 1964.

SCHUBERT, D. G.: *A Dictionary of Terms and Concepts in Reading.* Springfield, Thomas, 1964.

SCOTT, LOUISE B., and THOMPSON, J. J.: *Phonics in Listening, in Speaking, in Reading, in Writing.* St. Louis, McGraw (Webster Div.), 1962.

SEASHORE, H. G.: The Development of a Beam-Walking Test and its use in measuring development of balance in children. *Res Quart 18:* 246-259, 1947.

SEHON, ELIZABETH, and O'BRIEN, LOU: *Rhythms in Elementary Education.* New York, Ronald, 1951.

SIEGEL, E.: *Helping the Brain Injured Child.* New York, New York Association for Brain Injured Children, 1961.

SMALL, V. H.: *Ocular Pursuit Abilities and Readiness for Reading.* Doctoral dissertation, Purdue University, 1960.

SMITH, E. A.: *Reinforcement Psychology in Special Education.* Devon, Devereux Foundation, 1961.

SMITH, NILA B.: *American Reading Instruction.* Newark, International Reading Association, 1965.

SPACHE, G. D.: *Diagnostic Reading Scales.* Del Monte Research Park, California Test Bureau, 1963a.

SPACHE, G. D.: *Toward Better Reading.* Scarsdale (N.Y.), Garrard, 1963b.

SPERRY, BESSIE; ULRICH, D. N., and STAVER, NANCY: The relation of motility to boys' learning problems. *Amer J Orthopsychiat, 28:*640-646, 1958.

STANDING, E. M.: *Maria Montessori: Her Life and Work.* New York,

Mentor-Omega Books by New American Library of World Literature, 1957.

STANDING, E. M.: *The Montessori Method: A Revolution in Education.* Fresno, Academy Library Guild, 1962.

STEPHEN, ALBERTA: Quoted from a personal letter to Patrick Ashlock, December, 1967.

STERN, CATHERINE, and GOULD, TONI S.: *Children Discover Reading.* Syracuse, Random (Singer Div.), 1965.

STONE, C. R.: *The New Practice Readers.* New York, McGraw, 1962.

STRAUSS, A. A., and LEHTINEN, LAURA E.: *Psychopathology and Education of the Brain-Injured Child, Vol. I.* New York, Grune, 1947.

STRAUSS, A. A., and KEPHART, N. C.: *Psychopathology and Education of the Brain-Injured Child, Vol. II.* New York, Grune, 1965.

SZYPULA, G.: *Tumbling and Balancing for All.* Dubuque, Brown, 1957.

Teachall Reading Course: *Teachall Reading Course.* Washington, Publishers, 1962 .

Teaching Machines Inc.: *First Steps in Reading.* New York, Grolier (Teaching Materials Corp. Div.), 1962.

TERMAN, L. M., and MERRILL, MAUD A.: *Stanford-Binet Intelligence Scale.* Boston, Houghton, 1961.

THIESEN, W. W.: *Factors affecting results in primary reading. The Twentieth Yearb. Nat. Soc. Stud. Educ. Part II.* Bloomington, Public School Publishing, 1921.

THORPE, L. P.; CLARK, W. W., and TIEGS, E. W.: *California Test of Personality.* Del Monte Research Park, California Test Bureau, 1953.

TRAPP, E. P., and HIMELSTEIN, P. (EDS.): *Readings on the Exceptional Child.* New York, Appleton, 1962.

TYLER, R. W.: Educability and the schools. *Elem Sch J,* 49:200-212, 1948-1949.

UHL, W. L.: The use of the results of reading tests as a basis for planning remedial work. *Elem Sch J,* 17:273-280, 1916.

WATSON, F.: *The English Grammar Schools to 1660: Their Curriculum and Practice.* London, Cambridge U.P., 1908.

WATTENBERG, W. W.: *The Adolescent Years.* New York, Harcourt, 1955.

WEBB, J. R.: *Webb's Normal Reader, No. 3.* New York, New York, Sheldon, Lamport & Blakeman, 1856.

WECHSLER, D.: *Wechsler Intelligence Scale for Children.* New York, Psychological Corporation, 1949.

WECHSLER, D.: *Wechsler Adult Intelligence Scale.* New York, Psychological Corporation, 1955.

WECHSLER, D.: *Wechsler Preschool and Primary Scale of Intelligence.* New York, Psychological Corporation, 1966.

WEPMAN, J. M.: *Auditory Discrimination Test.* Chicago, Language Research Associates, 1958.

WERNER, H., and STRAUSS, A. A.: Types of visuo-motor activity in their relationship to low and high performance ages. *Proc Amer Assoc Ment Def 44*:163-168, 1939.

WILKINSON, C. B.: *Modern Physical Fitness.* New York, Viking, 1967.

WILLEE, A. W.: *Small Apparatus for Primary School Physical Education.* New York, Cambridge U.P., 1955.

WILSON, J. A., and ROBECK, MILDRED C.: *Kindergarten Evaluation of Learning Potential.* New York, McGraw, 1965.

WOOLLMAN, M.: *The Basal Progressive Choice Reading Program.* Washington, Institute for Education Research, 1962.

WOOD, NANCY E.: *Language Disorders in Children.* Chicago, National Society for Crippled Children and Adults, 1959.

YOAKAM, G. A.: *Report of the Eleventh Annual Conference on Reading.* Pittsburgh, The Reading Laboratory, School of Education, U. of Pittsburgh, 1955.

Appendix

Abelard-Schuman Ltd., 6 West Fifty-Seventh Street, New York, New York, 10019.

Abingdon Press, 201 Eighth Avenue, S., Nashville, Tennessee, 37202.

Academy Guild Press, 2430 East McKinley, Fresno, California, 93703.

Aladdin Books (See: American Book Company)

Allied Publishers, Inc., 645 Southeast Ankeny Street, Portland, Oregon, 97214.

American Association for Health, Recreation and Physical Education, 1201 Sixteenth Street, N. W., Washington, D. C., 20036.

American Book Company, 55 Fifth Avenue, New York, New York, 10003.

American Education Publications, Inc., Education Center, Columbus, Ohio, 43216.

American Educational Research Association, 1201 Sixteenth Street, N. W., Washington, D. C., 20036.

American Guidance Service, Inc., 720 Washington Avenue, S. E., Minneapolis, Minnesota, 55414.

Announcer Press, Luverne, Minnesota, 56156.

Appleton-Century-Crofts, Inc., Division of Meredith Publishing Company, 440 Park Avenue, S., New York, New York, 10016.

Argus Communications, 3505 North Ashland Avenue, Chicago, Illinois, 60657.

Ashlock Learning Center, P. O. Box 35132, Chicago, Illinois, 60635.

Association Instructional Materials, Division of Association Films, Inc., 347 Madison Avenue, New York, New York, 10017.

Atheneum Publishers, 162 East Thirty-Eighth Street, New York, New York, 10016.

Athletic Institute, 805 Merchandise Mart, Chicago, Illinois, 60654.

Barnell Loft Ltd., 111 South Centre Avenue, Rockville Centre, New York, 10013.

Basic Books, Inc., 404 Park Avenue, S., New York, New York, 10016.

Beckley-Cardy Company, 1900 North Narragansett Avenue, Chicago, Illinois, 60639.

Behavioral Research Laboratories, P. O. Box 577, Palo Alto, California, 94302.

Benefic Press (See: Beckley-Cardy Company)

Bentley (Robert), Inc., 872 Massachusetts Avenue, Cambridge, Massachusetts, 02139.

Bobbs-Merrill Company, Inc., 4300 West Sixty-Second Street, Indianapolis, Indiana, 46206.

Bremner-Davis, 511 Fourth Street, Wilmette, Illinois, 60091.

Brown, (Wm. C.), 135 South Locust Street, Dubuque, Iowa, 52001.

Burdette & Company, 437 D Street, Boston, Massachusetts, 02210.

Burgess Publishing Company, 426 South Street, Minneapolis, Minnesota, 55415.

California State Department of Education, Sacramento, California, 93706.

California Test Bureau, Division of McGraw-Hill Book Company, Del Monte Research Park, Monterey, California, 93940.

Cambridge University Press, 32 East Fifty-Seventh Street, New York, New York, 10022.

Carson (Esther O.), 18623 Lake Chabot Road, Castro Valley, California, 94546.

Catholic University of America Press, 620 Michigan Avenue, N. E., Washington, D. C., 20017.

CENCO Educational Aids, Cenco Center, 2600 South Kostner Avenue, Chicago, Illinois, 60623.

Center for Applied Research in Education, Inc., 7 Fifth Avenue, New York, New York, 10011.

Chester Electronic Laboratories, Inc., Chester, Connecticut, 06412.

Childrens Press, Inc., Jackson Boulevard and Ravine Avenue, Chicago, Illlinois, 60607.

Committee on Diagnostic Reading Tests, Mountain Home, North Carolina, 28758.

Community Playthings, Rifton, New York, 12471.

Consulting Psychologists Press, 577 College Avenue, Palo Alto, California, 94306.

Continental Press, Inc., Elizabethtown, Pennsylvania, 17022.

Coronet Films, 65 East South Water Street, Chicago, Illinois, 60601.

Coward-McCann, Inc., 200 Madison Avenue, New York, New York, 10016.

Creative Playthings, Princeton, New Jersey, 08540.

Crowell-Collier Publishing Company, 640 Fifth Avenue, New York, New York, 10019.

Daigger & Company, 159 West Kinzie Street, Chicago, Illinois, 60610.

Day (John) Company, 62 West Forty-Fifth Street, New York, New York, 10036.

Denison (T. S.) & Company, Inc., 315 Fifth Avenue, S., Minneapolis, Minnesota, 55415.

Devereux Foundation, Devon, Pennsylvania, 19333.

Dial Press, 750 Third Avenue, New York, New York, 10017.

Doubleday & Company, Inc., 501 Franklin Avenue, Garden City, New York, 11531.

Dutton (E. P.) & Company, Inc., 201 Park Avenue, S., New York, New York, 10003.

Economy Company, 5811 West Minnesota, Indianapolis, Indiana, 46241.

Educational Activities, Inc., Freeport, New York, 11520.

Educational Aids, 845 Wisteria Drive, Fremont, California, 94538.

Educational Developmental Laboratories, 284 East Pulaski Road, Huntington, New York, 11743.

Educational Recording Service, 5922 Abernathy Drive, Los Angeles, California, 90045.

Educational Research Associates, Inc., P. O. Box 6604, Philadelphia, Pennsylvania, 19149.

Educational Testing Service, Princeton, New Jersey, 08540.

Educators Publishing Service, 301 Vassar Street, Cambridge, Massachusetts, 02139.

Essay Press, P. O. Box 5, Planetarium Station, New York, New York, 10024.

Follett Publishing Company, 1010 West Washington Boulevard, Chicago, Illinois, 60607.

Garden City Books (See: Doubleday and Company)

Garrard Publishing Company, Champaign, Illinois, 61820.

Gilbert Press, Inc., (See: Messner)

Ginn & Company, Statler Building, Back Bay, P. O. Box 191, Boston, Massachusetts, 02117.

Globe Book Company, 175 Fifth Avenue, New York, New York, 10010.

Golden Press, Inc., 850 Third Avenue, New York, New York, 10022.

Grossett & Dunlap, Inc., 51 Madison Avenue, New York, New York, 10010.

Grune & Stratton, Inc., 381 Fourth Avenue, New York, New York, 10016.

Gryphon Press, 220 Montgomery Street, Highland Park, New Jersey, 08904.

Hale (E. M.) & Company, 1201 South Hastings Way, Eau Claire, Wisconsin, 54702.

Hamilton Publishing Company, Inc., 224 West Tenth Street, Larned, Kansas, 67550.

Hammett (J. L.) Company, 2393 Vauxhall Road, Union, New Jersey, 07083.

Harper & Row, Publishers, El-Hi Division, 2500 Crawford Avenue, Evanston, Illinois, 60201.

Harr Wagner Publishing Company, 609 Mission Street, San Francisco, California, 94105.

Harvard University Press, Kittridge Hall, 79 Garden Street, Cambridge, Massachusetts, 02138.

Hastings House Publishers, Inc., 151 East Fiftieth Street, New York, New York, 10022.

Heath (D. C.) & Company, 285 Columbus Avenue, Boston, Massachusetts, 02116.

Hoeber Medical Division, Harper & Row Publishers, 49 East Thirty-Third Street, New York, New York, 10016.

Holiday House, 8 West Thirteenth Street, New York, New York, 10011.

Holt, Rinehart & Winston, Inc., 383 Madison Avenue, New York, New York, 10017.

Houghton Mifflin Company, Educational Division, 110 Tremont Street, Boston, Massachusetts, 02107.

Humanities Press, Inc., 303 Park Avenue, S., New York, New York, 10010.

Hunter College, 695 Park Avenue, New York, New York, 10021.

Ideal School Supply Company, 11000 South Lavergne Avenue, Oaklawn, Illinois, 60453.

Illinois Curriculum Program, Office of the Superintendent of Public Instruction, 302 State Office Building, Springfield, Illinois, 62706.

International Reading Association, 6 Tyre Avenue, Newark, Delaware, 19711.

Johns Hopkins Press, Baltimore, Maryland, 21218.

Kalakshetra Publications, Adyar, Madras 20, India*

Keystone View Company, Subsidiary of Mast Development Company, Meadville, Pennsylvania, 16335.

Knoph (Alfred A.), Inc., 501 Madison Avenue, New York, New York, 10022.

Laidlaw Brothers, Division of Doubleday & Company, Inc., Thatcher and Madison Streets, River Forest, Illinois, 60305.

Language Research Associates, P. O. Box 95, 950 East Fifty-Ninth Street, Chicago, Illinois, 60637.

Lathrop, Norman Enterprises, P. O. Box 83, Flint, Michigan, 48501.

Lea & Febiger, 600 South Washington Square, Philadelphia, Pennsylvania, 19106.

---

*Distributed in the U. S. by The Theosophical Press, P. O. Box 270, Wheaton, Illinois, 60188.

Lippincott (J. B.) Company, East Washington Square, Philadelphia, Pennsylvania, 19105.

Little, Brown & Company, 34 Beacon Street, Boston, Massachusetts, 02106.

Liveright Publishing Corporation, 386 Park Avenue, S., New York, New York, 10016.

Longmans, Green & Company, Inc., 119 West Fortieth Street, New York, New York, 10018.

Lyons & Carnahan, Affiliate of Meredith Publishing Company, 407 East Twenty-Fifth Street, Chicago, Illinois, 60616.

McGraw-Hill Book Company, 330 West Forty-Second Street, New York, New York, 10036.

McKay (David) Company, Inc., 750 Third Avenue, New York, New York, 10017.

Macmillan Company, Subsidiary of Crowell, Collier & Macmillan, Inc., 866 Third Avenue, New York, New York, 10022.

McQueen Publishing Company, P. O. Box 198, Tiskilwa, Illinois, 61368.

Macrae Smith Company, 225 South Fifteenth Street, Philadelphia, Pennsylvania, 19102.

Mafex Associates, Inc., P. O. Box 519, Johnstown, Pennsylvania, 15907.

Martin Publishing Company, P. O. Box 1012, San Diego, California, 92112.

Mentor Press, 360 West Twenty-Third Street, New York, New York, 10011.

Merrill (Charles E.) Books, 1300 Alum Creek Drive, Columbus, Ohio, 43216.

Messner (Julian), Inc., 1 West Thirty-Ninth Street, New York, New York, 10018.

Mills Center, 1512 East Broward Boulevard, Fort Lauderdale, Florida, 33301.

Milton Bradley Company, 74 Park Street, Springfield, Massachusetts, 01105

Morrow (William) & Company, Inc., 425 Park Avenue, S., New York, New York, 10016.

Mosby (C. V.) Company, 3207 Washington Boulevard, St. Louis, Missouri, 63103.

National Society for Crippled Children and Adults, 11 South LaSalle Street, Chicago, Illinois, 60603.

Nelson (Thomas) & Sons, Copewood & Davis Streets, Camden, New Jersey, 08103.

New Jersey Department of Public Instruction, Trenton, New Jersey, 08625.

New Readers Press, P. O. Box 131, Syracuse, New York, 13210.

New York Association for Brain Injured Children, 305 Broadway, New York, New York, 10007.

New York Times, Times Square, New York, New York, 10021.

O'Connor Reading Clinic Publishing Company, 772 East Maple Road, Birmingham, Michigan, 48011.

Odyssey Press, Text Department, 55 Fifth Avenue, New York, New York, 10003.

Orient Longmans, Ltd., 17 Chittaranjan Avenue, Calcutta, 13, India.*

Oxford University Press, Inc., 417 Fifth Avenue, New York, New York, 10016.

Paine Publishing Company, 34 North Jefferson Street, Dayton, Ohio, 45401.

Pantheon Books, Inc., 22 East Fifty-First Street, New York, New York, 10022.

Parkinson (R. W.) and Associates, (See Follett Publishing Co.)

Parnassus Press, 2422 Ashby Avenue, Berkeley, California, 94705.

Pergamon Press, Inc., 44-01 Twenty-First Street, Long Island, New York, 11101.

Phonovisual Products, Inc., P. O. Box 5625, Washington, D. C., 20016.

Pocket Books, Inc., 630 Fifth Avenue, New York, New York, 10020.

Portal Press, Inc., Publishers, 369 Lexington Avenue, New York, New York, 10017.

Prentice-Hall, Inc., Englewood Cliffs, New Jersey, 07632.

Princeton University Press, Princeton, New Jersey, 08541.

Psychological Corporation, 304 East Forty-Fifth Street, New York, New York, 10017.

Public School Publishing Company, 204 West Mulberry Street, Bloomington, Illinois, 61701.

Public School Publishing Company, 345 Calhoun Street, Cincinnati, Ohio, 45219.

Publishers Company, Inc., 1250 Connecticut Avenue, N. W., Washington, D. C., 20036.

Purdue University Studies, West Lafayette, Indiana, 47906.

Putnam's (G. P.) Sons, 200 Madison Avenue, New York, New York, 10016.

Quadrangle Books, Inc., 180 North Wacker Drive, Chicago, Illinois, 60606.

Random House, Inc., 457 Madison Avenue, New York, New York, 10022.

---

*Distributed in the U. S. by The Theosophical Press, P. O. Box 270, Wheaton, Illinois, 60188.

Reading Laboratory, School of Education, University of Pittsburgh, Pittsburgh, Pennsylvania, 15213.

Regnery (Henry) Company, 114 West Illinois Street, Chicago, Illinois, 60610.

Rehabilitation Center, 8801 Stenton Avenue, Philadelphia, Pennsylvania, 19118.

Reilly & Lee Company (See: Regnery)

Richards (Frank E.), Publisher, Phoenix, New York, 13135.

Ronald Press Company, 15 East Twenty-Sixth Street, New York, New York, 10010.

St. Martin's Press, Inc., 175 Fifth Avenue, New York, New York, 10010.

Sanborn (Benjamin H.) & Company (See: Singer (L. W.), Inc.)

Schocken Books, Inc., 67 Park Avenue, New York, New York, 10016.

Scholastic Magazines, Inc., 50 West Forty-Fourth Street, New York, New York, 10036.

School Playthings, Inc., 1801 South Michigan Avenue, Chicago, Illinois, 60616.

Science Research Associates, Inc., 259 East Erie Street, Chicago, Illinois, 60611.

Scott (William R.), Inc., 333 Avenue of the Americas, New York, New York, 10014.

Scott, Foresman & Company, 1900 East Lake Avenue, Glenview, Illinois, 60025.

Scribner's (Charles) Sons, 597 Fifth Avenue, New York, New York, 10017.

Silver Burdett Company, Division of General Learning Corporation, Morrison, New Jersey, 07960.

Singer (L. W.), Inc., Subsidiary of Random House, Inc., 249-259 West Erie Boulevard, Syracuse, New York, 13202.

Special Child Publications, 71 Columbia Street, Seattle, Washington, 98104.

Stanwix House, Inc., 3020 Chartiers Avenue, Pittsburgh, Pennsylvania, 15204.

Steck-Vaughn Company, P. O. Box 2028, Austin, Texas, 78761.

Sterling Publishing Company, Inc., 419 Park Avenue, S., New York, New York, 10016.

Stone, (R. H.) Products, P. O. Box 414, Detroit, Michigan, 48231.

Syracuse University Press, P. O. Box 87, University Station, Syracuse, New York, 13210.

Taplinger Publishing Company, Inc., 29 East Tenth Street, New York, New York, 10003.

Teachers College Press, Columbia University, 525 West One Hundred Twentieth Street, New York, New York, 10027.

Teaching Resources, Educational Service of The New York Times, 334 Boylston Street, Boston, Massachusetts, 02116.

Theosophical Publishing House, Adyar, Madras 20, India.*

Thomas (Charles C), Publisher, 301-327 East Lawrence Avenue, Springfield, Illinois, 62703.

U. S. Government Printing Office, Washington, D. C., 20402.

University of Chicago Press, 5750 Ellis Avenue, Chicago, Illinois, 60637.

University of Illinois Press, Urbana, Illinois, 61801.

University Microfilms, Inc., 313 North First Street, Ann Arbor, Michigan, 48106.

Vantage Press, 1946 Vedanta Place, Hollywood, California, 90028.

Viking Press, 625 Madison Avenue, New York, New York, 10022.

Wahr (George Publishing Company, 316 South State Street, Ann Arbor, Michigan, 48108.

Walck (Henry Z.), 101 Fifth Avenue, New York, New York, 10003.

Watts (Franklin) Inc., Subsidiary of Grolier, 575 Lexington Avenue, New York, New York, 10022.

Webster Division, McGraw-Hill Book Company, Manchester Road, Manchester, Missouri, 63011.

Westminister Press, Witherspoon Building, Philadelphia, Pennsylvania, 19107.

Whitman (Albert) & Company, 560 West Lake Street, Chicago, Illinois, 60606.

Wiley (John) & Sons, Inc., 605 Third Avenue, New York, New York, 10016.

William & Wilkins Company, 428 East Preston Street, Baltimore, Maryland, 21202.

Winston (John) Company, 1010 Arch Street, Philadelphia, Pennsylvania, 19107.

World Publishing Company, Subsidiary of Times Mirror Company, 2231 West One Hundred Tenth Street, Cleveland, Ohio, 44102.

---

*Distributed in the U. S. by The Theosophical Press, P. O. Box 270, Wheaton, Illinois, 60188.

Name Index*

*See Chapter 7 for names of authors of instructional materials.

Reference Index*

*See Chapter 7 for titles of instructional materials.

Subject Index

A

ABC books, 31
Accent, 96
Achievement Center for Children, 66
Activity Movement, 30
Aggressiveness, 23
Aggressive behavior disorder, 19
Augmented Roman Alphabet, 97. *See also* Initial Teaching Alphabet
Alexia, ix, 38
Alphabet, 34, 42, 97, 98
Alphabet method, 31, 35
Anxiety, x, 53
Aphasia, viii, 20, 40
Aphasiod syndrome, 19
Association deficit pathology, 18
Association for Children with Learning Disabilities, 57, 162
Attention disorders, 19
Audiometry, 67

B

Basal readers, 30
Behavior, 20, 65
Bibliotherapy, 40
Blending, 79, 81. *See also* Word attack skills
Blends, 80, 93. *See also* Word attack skills
Board of Education, 150, 151
Body flexibility, 85
Body image, 23, 83
Body movement, 83
Borderline subnormals, 47
Brain injured children, 20, 24, 50, 59, 161
Brain injury, viii, 40
Build-up, 52, 81-88
Build-up materials, 108-111

C

Catastrophic reactions, 23
Causation, 23, 25, 47, 160. *See also* Etiology
Cerebral dominancy, 40
Cerebral dysfunction, 18
Cerebral dys-synchronization syndrome, 18
Cerebral palsy, 20
Character impulse disorder, 19
Choreiform syndrome, 18
Clinic, reading, 143
Clumsy child syndrome, 19
Cognition, 76
Comprehension, 5, 13, 14, 28, 29, 36, 38, 40, 41, 81, 105, 106, 113, 114
  in depth, 5, 14, 15
  literal, 5, 14
Compound words, 95. *See also* Word attack skills
Concept burden, 158
Conceptual difficulties, 23
Conceptually handicapped, 19
Configuration, 80, 90, 91. *See also* Word recognition
Consonants, 80, 81, 93, 95. *See also* Work attack skills
Context clues, 90. *See also* Word recognition
Corrective instruction, x, 5-7, 26, 159
Council for Exceptional Children, 17, 162
Cove Schools, 50, 59
Cultural deprivation, 20
Culturally disadvantaged, 17
Custodians, 146

D

Daydreaming, 23
Delinquency, 47, 48